School Superintendents:
Careers and Performance

School Superintendents:
Careers and Performance

RICHARD O. CARLSON

Center for the Advanced Study of
Educational Administration
University of Oregon

CHARLES E. MERRILL PUBLISHING COMPANY

A Bell & Howell Company
Columbus, Ohio

MERRILL'S SERIES FOR EDUCATIONAL ADMINISTRATION

Under the Editorship of

DR. LUVERN L. CUNNINGHAM, Dean

College of Education
The Ohio State University

and

DR. H. THOMAS JAMES, President

The Spencer Foundation
Chicago, Illinois

This work was developed under a contract from the U.S. Office of Education, Department of Health, Education and Welfare. However, opinions expressed herein do not necessarily reflect the position or policy of that Agency, and no official endorsement should be inferred.

International Standard Book Number: 0–675–09165–9

Library of Congress Catalog Card Number: 72–175818

1 2 3 4 5 6 7 8 9 10 – 76 75 74 73 72

PRINTED IN THE UNITED STATES OF AMERICA

Preface

The term *career* ordinarily refers to the unfolding sequence of jobs or positions within an occupation through which an individual moves. A career can be viewed from at least two broad perspectives. One view holds the individuals who are tracing out a career at the center of interest. Attention is given to matters such as the factors which contribute to one's occupational choice and career decisions; the ways in which competencies, aspirations, and the like are related to the development of the career; the means by which individuals promote their own careers; and how they climb the occupational ladder with what strategies and through what career stages. The other view holds the job at the center of interest. Questions are raised about the impact on the job, surrounding jobs, and the containing organization as individuals under varying circumstances move in and out of it. "Executive succession" is the term applied to the latter perspective. These two perspectives are not unrelated. The way in which an individual manages to trace out a career has considerable bearing on the way in which he manages himself and his work as he assumes a new post.

The notion of career is the main theme of this study. The dual perspective, after a fashion, has been utilized in the analysis. Over-all, an attempt has been made to show how career factors of chief managers of public education relate to the way in which they function once in office.

This orientation was, by and large, accidental—at least the outcome was somewhat different from the original intention. My original intention was to concentrate on the way in which a chief executive new to his post related to the social structure of the containing organization. I was curious about the constraints that the social structure of an ongoing organization might place on a successor and the ways in which a successor would adapt to these constraints. And it was assumed that succession, with its natural dislocating features, would bring into sharp relief the relationship between an executive and the social structure of the organization. As matters turned out, little attention was devoted to this issue. Nevertheless the first brush with the general problem resulted in a monograph published in 1962 titled *Executive Succession and Organizational Change*. The present volume is an outgrowth and extension of that report.

No one urged me to extend the analysis to its present form, for which I am grateful. However, in the process of so doing, many people aided in many ways; and to them I wish to acknowledge indebtedness and express appreciation.

Richard O. Carlson

September 23, 1971

Contents

School Superintendents:

Careers and Performance

1

Executive Succession

With the cartoonist's ability to capture the essence of the human situation, Bill Mauldin depicts in the drawing on the following page some important truths about the army.[1] What he implies about the army applies in general to organizations. First he shows us that the army is not totally dependent on the individual; the army has obviously survived beyond the life span of the lieutenant's predecessor. However, as the cartoon suggests, to survive an organization must cope with the continual problem of making replacements in its series of offices. By and large, replacing an individual is a routine affair. For example, little thought is ordinarily given to replacing a freight-elevator operator. But replacing a person in a key position is another matter. When an important office is involved, the event's significance is obvious. It is clearly brought home forcefully, as at the beginning of F. D. R.'s term as President or when a family takes in a new man.

---

[1] Bill Mauldin, *Up Front* (Cleveland, Ohio: World Publishing Co., 1945). Drawings copyrighted 1944 by United Features Syndicate, Inc. Reproduced by courtesy of Bill Mauldin.

*"By th' way, what wuz them changes you wuz gonna make
when you took over last month, sir?"*

Besides indicating that an organization persists beyond the life of any of its members and that an organization must cope with making replacements, the cartoon tells us something about the replacement process. The fact Willie raised a question may indicate that he had had misgivings about serving under a new man; he felt uncomfortable about the establishment of a new working relationship. This indicates that the replacing of an executive is a potentially disruptive event. At one extreme, the event can be traumatic. Executive succession often disrupts lines of authority and communication, disturbs power and decision-making systems, and generally upsets the organization's normal activities. At the least, executive succession dislocates several persons from their normal relationships with the organization, creating the additional disruptive, if not painful, problem of relocating.

Willie's question deals with change. His concern indicates that executive succession often precedes further organizational adaptation, development, and change. In fact, this is often the reason for the replacement of executives. The proverb "a new broom sweeps clean" indicates the relationship between executive succession and organizational change.

Mauldin's cartoon, then, implies three ideas: an enduring organization must cope with the continual need of making replacements; when key positions are involved, the process of replacing individuals can be disruptive; and, the replacement process may influence organizational adaptation and development.

Organizations must frequently adapt to succession and its developmental significance and potential disruptive character; thus, as a process, it deserves close examination. Organization theory must contain propositions about succession, organizational responses of succession, and organizational consequences of succession.[2]

In spite of, or perhaps because of, the frequent occurrence of executive succession in formal organizations, it has received little systematic study. Some rather interesting questions can be raised, however, about this type of event. What strategies are available to a successor in making the kind of changes the lieutenant had in mind? What problems confront successors as they try to deal with an organization? What tactics can be employed by personnel such as Willie, Joe, and their friends to block or curtail the development of the lieutenant's plans? Does the social structure of the group experiencing executive succession have an impact on the consequences of succession? Do the personal factors and sociological circumstances of the individual successor play a part in the consequences of succession? Does the fact that the lieutenant failed to make changes influence the decision about who should be his successor?

In a sense this account expands on the points made in Mauldin's cartoon, for it seeks to answer the types of questions raised above. The questions, however, are generated within the context of the public

---

[2] The meager systematic literature concerned with succession and its consequences is for the most part descriptive in nature and tends to overplay the disruptive aspects. Propositions are seldom developed or tested. There are, however, notable exceptions. Trow has tested some propositions about succession rates in small groups, and Scheff has attempted to account for individual differences in regard to the resistance to change that frequently follows succession. See Donald B. Trow, "Membership Succession and Team Performance," *Human Relations,* Vol. 13 (August, 1960), 259–68; and Thomas J. Scheff, "Perceptual Orientation of Staff Members Toward Patients in a Mental Hospital Ward," paper read at the American Sociological Association meeting, August, 1960.

school system; and the inquiry centers on the executive position of the school superintendent.

ANALYTICAL FRAMEWORK:
THE NATURAL HISTORY OF THE SUCCESSION CYCLE

No attempt is made here to analyze the whole problem of executive succession. This presentation is selective in character. An attempt has been made to reveal the basic patterns by which types of successors relate to their containing organizations. In part, this means that attention is focused on the central patterns of motivation and the action of various kinds of successors. But to indicate that a central pattern of action for all kinds of successors exists by no means suggests that individuals do not deviate from it. Over-all, the data are focused on the adaptation between the chief executive official and the organization; the analysis seeks to draw out the organizational consequences of that adaptation.

This analysis is ordered in terms of the natural history of the succession cycle. That cycle starts with the decision to seek a successor to replace the chief executive and ends with the decision to obtain a successor for the successor. First, the organization faces the prospect of replacing its chief executive. This prompts or intensifies the assessment of the organizational situation; thus some judgments are made about the state of affairs, and some notions are formulated about the course the organization should take. These judgments and notions then influence the type of successor chosen and the conditions of his employment. Men are interviewed; one is hired. The successor takes over, engages in certain activities, and avoids others; and thus he leads the organization down a course. But the successor does not last forever. At the end of his stay, the organization again faces the prospect of obtaining a successor. The past performance is judged. The situation is reassessed. The performance turned in by the first successor determines decisions about the organizational course and, therefore, about the next successor. Thus the circle is complete. The chapters that follow are organized around this sequence of unfolding events.

Chapters 2, 3, 4, and 5 deal with successors, beginning with an overview of some of the characteristics of school superintendents, who are at the center of the study. Chapter 2 notes several career contingencies of the superintendency. Chapter 3 identifies two main kinds of successors, career-bound and place-bound, and depicts some of their basic characteristics and commitments. Analysis of the nature of the two types of successors reveals their central patterns of motivation. Chapter 4 describes the characteristics and commitments that bear on the careers of the two kinds of school superintendents. This chapter discusses career decisions, preparation for the career, and career orientations; it reveals basic differences in the tendencies of the two types. Chapter 5 also depicts differences between the two by showing how career- and place-bound men are differentially placed in the social structure of school superintendents.

Chapter 6 moves to the next stage of the succession cycle and indicates the circumstances that lead an organization to select a career-bound or place-bound executive as a successor. The chapter also specifies some of the factors that determine the terms of employment for the two types of successors, and points out how these employment conditions influence performance.

The next three chapters show the organizational consequences of employment of the one type rather than the other by portraying the performances of place-bound and career-bound successors. Chapter 7 shows how their performances differ regarding the attention they give to policy and how these differences influence the course down which they are leading the organization. Chapter 8 describes some differences with respect to the relationship that develops between the executives and their work forces. Chapter 9 examines performance of successors regarding the educational program by showing how they respond differently to the opportunity to adopt educational innovations. In these three chapters, place-bound and career-bound successors are dealt with simultaneously; and the contrast in their performances indicates the differences in the directions they move their organizations. These chapters focus on the successors' first few years in office, for they seem to be decisive in setting a pattern.

Chapter 10 picks up the unfolding events at the end of the stay in office. It specifies the factors that bear upon the length of stay in office of the two types and what this time period means for organizational development.

The analysis is brought full cycle in Chapter 11, which summarizes what the terms in office of place-bound and career-bound executives mean for organizational development and, through an examination of succession patterns, shows how the performance of a successor is related to the selection of his successor.

2

Career Contingencies

Before embarking on the detailed discussion of types of successors, their career styles, their conditions of employment, and their performance, it is appropriate to pause and look at the men in the focus of this study—the school superintendents. It is desirable to note some of their characteristics which distinguish them from other occupational groups, for after all only the occupation of housewife "... shows approximately the same distribution of intelligence and of all aptitudes as the general population." [1] Guiding the look at the superintendents will be the notion of career contingencies. Entry into an occupation and movement through an occupational structure, social system, or hierarchy is contingent on circumstances, skills, attitudes, and among other things, acquired and ascribed attributes. Here we want to search out and identify some of the contingencies of the superintendency.

---

[1] Theodore Caplow, *The Sociology of Work* (New York: McGraw-Hill Book Company, 1954), p. 260.

THE CAREER LADDER

The ladder of assent to the superintendency is not very long or intricate. The principle positions in the public schools are teacher, principal, and superintendent. In larger school systems, there may be a number of positions standing between the superintendent and the principals, such as directors, supervisors, or coordinators of personnel, curriculum, secondary schools, elementary schools, and finance. These positions sometimes carry the title of Assistant Superintendent. Occupational specialization in the schools is meager, as differentiation has not developed as rapidly or as extensively as in most other professions. Given the degree of occupational specialization in schools today, it might be said that the situation is comparable to trying to manage the contemporary American economy with only the occupational classifications and specializations that existed in Europe in the sixteenth century. As an article in a recent issue of *Forbes* points out, education is "the last of the big handwork industries." The lack of occupational specialization causes a blurring of demarkation between line positions and staff positions. Few positions in the schools are clearly staff positions. Thus movement up the hierarchy is not strictly a matter of movement up through line positions. Staff positions are not dead ends. As school people climb the ladder they tend to move back and forth between quasi-line and staff positions.

To be a school superintendent, according to the regulations in virtually every state, one must have been a classroom teacher. Male classroom teachers are in the minority; 90 per cent of all elementary school teachers are women and 60 per cent of all high school teachers are female.[2] Though they are seriously outnumbered, men move to school administrative posts more frequently than women. It has been estimated that the chances of movement to administrative posts is seven to ten times greater for men.[3] The stronghold for women is the elementary school principalship; even in that post two-thirds to three-fourths of the occupants are males and the number of females seems to be declining.[4] Moreover, school teachers drop out of the occupation in large numbers. Among men teaching in 1956, less than 10 per cent of

---

[2] Orville G. Brim, Jr., *Sociology and the Field of Education* (New York: Russell Sage Foundation, 1958), p. 30.

[3] C. N. Morris, "Career Patterns of Teachers," in L. Stiles (ed.), *The Teacher's Role in American Society* (New York: Harper & Row, Publishers, 1957), chapter 18.

[4] Myron Lieberman, *Education as a Profession* (Englewood Cliffs, N.J.: Prentice-Hall, Inc., 1956), p. 243.

them had been teaching for five or more years.[5] Thus, the male teaching force from which superintendents are drawn, compared to the female teaching force, is small; and this relatively small force is reduced drastically and quickly by those leaving the occupation.

Because men are very much in the minority in public schools, because their ranks are rapidly depleted by those dropping out of the occupation, and because they are advanced to administrative posts far more frequently than women, the men who simply persist in the occupation have a high probability of moving up the ladder. Thus, sheer *perseverance* seems to be a contingency of the superintendency: perseverance in an occupation that is highly feminized and in which men suffer "psychological and financial deprivation." [6]

Because occupational specialization in the schools is meager, the ordinary career traces left by school superintendents as they rise to the position are uncomplicated. The usual career trace is teacher-principal-superintendent. Superintendents in the very small systems frequently by-pass the principalship. Those who hold the post in the larger systems have frequently held a directorship or an assistant superintendency which gave them system-wide responsibility and experience. In this generally uncomplicated trace from teacher to principal to superintendent, association with elementary schools seems partially to block movement to the superintendency; the elementary school principalship seems especially to be a dead end for those aspiring to the superintendency.[7]

Of greater importance than the career trace is the process by which movement up the ladder from teacher to superintendent is achieved. However, information about the process among superintendents is virtually non-existent. Griffiths has reported that teachers who aspire to other positions extensively engage in practices designed to get the attention of their superiors; and Blood has indicated that teachers desiring to be principals systematically and consciously study the job of the principal as it is played out by the principal in the building in which they work.[8] Whatever the process used to climb the ladder, it is

---

[5] Burton R. Clark, "Sociology of Education," in R. E. L. Faris (ed.), *Handbook of Modern Sociology* (Chicago: Rand McNally & Co., 1964), p. 754.

[6] *Ibid.*, p. 756.

[7] See Eugene Dils, "How Administrators Climb the Ladder," *The School Executive*, Vol. 74 (September, 1954), 62–63; and Clyde Morris, "Careers of 554 Public School Superintendents in Eleven Midwest States" (Ph.D. diss., University of Wisconsin, 1957).

[8] See Daniel E. Griffiths, *et al.*, "Teacher Mobility in New York City," *Educational Administration Quarterly*, Vol. 1 (Winter, 1965), 15–31; and Ronald E. Blood, "The Function of Experience in Professional Preparation: Teaching and

clear that sponsorship plays a substantial part for many.[9]

Age is a contingency in the superintendency as it is in many occupations. Many surveys have reported that 50 is about the average age of superintendents and that they enter the position for the first time during their early forties. Attitudes of school board members confirm the desirability of men assuming the superintendency while in their forties. When asked to specify preferred age ranges in hiring a new superintendent, a large sample of Massachusetts school board members showed a clear preference for the age range of 40 to 49. Forty-four per cent of the sample thought the new superintendent should be in that age range and only 2 per cent thought that he should not. In descending order, the age ranges preferred were: 40–49; 30–39; 50–59; and 60 and older.[10] The negative views expressed by school board members about hiring superintendents who are 50 and older strongly suggest that the superintendency held by men over 50 is probably the terminal superintendency. Data supporting this contention can be seen in Figure 2–1, which shows the percentage of superintendents in various age groups among a national sample who were in the first year in office of their current superintendency.

Once a man has obtained a superintendency the career ladder does not end. Superintendencies differ drastically, and there is considerable interest in moving to a different superintendency among superintendents: about 40 per cent indicate they are very or somewhat interested in moving to a new superintendency. The interest does not decline as the number of superintendencies held increases.[11] This high interest, in part, leads to substantial intraoccupational mobility. A national sample indicates that about 26 per cent have held two superintendencies, 14 per cent have held three, 9 per cent have held four, and 7 per cent have held five or more superintendencies.[12]

In that school superintendencies differ, they can be ordered in terms of their prestige. To a considerable extent, prestige of the superintendency held defines success among school superintendents. Prestige of

---

the Principalship" (Ph.D. diss., Claremont Graduate School, 1966). On a more general plane, see William R. Dill, *et al.*, "How Aspiring Managers Promote their Own Careers," *California Management Review*, Vol. 2 (Summer, 1960), 9–15.

[9] Robert L. Rose, "Career Sponsorship in the School Superintendency" (Ph.D. diss., University of Oregon, 1969).

[10] See Neal Gross, *et al.*, *Explorations in Role Analysis* (New York: John Wiley & Sons, Inc., 1958), pp. 335, 337, 338.

[11] R. J. Snow and Edward S. Hickcox, "National Study of School Superintendents," 1967.

[12] American Association of School Administrators, *Profile of the Superintendent* (Washington, D.C., 1960), p. 82.

the superintendency might be "determined by its standing on three general types of criteria: first, *managerial responsibility* as measured

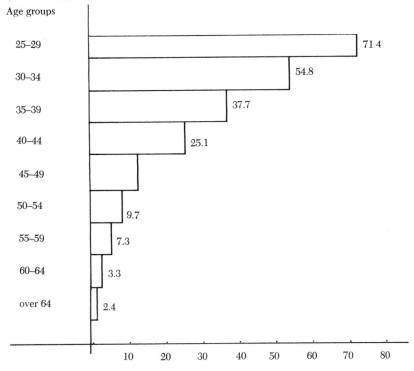

Per cent of superintendents in first year in office of superintendency

Figure 2–1

AGE AND TENURE IN OFFICE

by the size of the organization; second, the *quality* of the school system in terms of 'professional standards'; and third, the *facilities* available to the incumbent of the position," reason Mason and Gross as they work out the matter of prestige of the superintendencies in Massachusetts.[13] Their reasoning, as is evident, flows from the assumption that prestige of a given superintendency is a function of the opportunity afforded in the position to contribute to education. However, regardless of the nice logic of the assumption and its high principles,

[13] Ward S. Mason and Neal Gross, "Intra-Occupational Prestige Differentiation: The School Superintendency," *American Sociological Review*, Vol. 20 (June, 1955), 328.

the findings made it clear that "the working hypothesis must be rejected. The best prediction of prestige is obtained *not* by using variables which measure the opportunity to contribute to the function of the position, but by using a single variable, salary." [14]

Having noted that the prestige structure of the occupation is graded by salary, which is strongly related to school system size,[15] we can see to what extent the career of the superintendent is graded by age and intraoccupational mobility. One might assume that the most prestigious superintendencies would be held by the senior members of the occupation and Table 2–1 indicates the extent to which this is true. It shows, by and large, that the higher the prestige of the superintendency (as measured by system size), the greater the tendency for the position holder to be over 50 years old.

Table 2–1

PRESTIGE AND AGE OF SUPERINTENDENTS

PRESTIGE (System size from small to large)	AGE (Percentage of superintendents 49 and younger)
1	66%
2	63
3	54
4	52
5	44
6	25
7	47
8	16

Source: Secondary analysis of data from R. J. Snow and Edward S. Hickcox, "National Study of School Superintendents," 1967.

Similarly, one might assume that the most prestigious superintendencies would be held by the superintendents with the greatest amount of experience in the position, those who had held several superintendencies. Table 2–2 shows the mean salary (prestige) of over 1,100 superintendents by the number of superintendencies held. While the occupation seems to be graded according to age, it is clearly not definitely graded according to experience in a number of superinten-

---

[14] *Ibid.*, p. 330.
[15] *Ibid.*, p. 329.

dencies. Those in the second superintendency earn a somewhat higher salary (and thus have higher prestige) than those in the first superintendency. Beyond one move, however, gaining experience in a number of superintendencies does not lead to more prestigious positions.

Table 2–2

PRESTIGE AND NUMBER OF SUPERINTENDENCIES HELD

NUMBER OF SUPERINTENDENCIES HELD	PRESTIGE (Mean Salary)
1	$13,358
2	$14,361
3	$14,445
4 or more	$14,455

Source: Secondary analysis of data from R. J. Snow and Edward S. Hickcox, "National Study of School Superintendents," 1967.

The most prestigious positions are not held by the men who have occupied a number of different superintendencies.

The fact that the occupation is not graded according to experience in a number of superintendencies indicates that much of the intraoccupational mobility of superintendents is *horizontal* career mobility (from one superintendency to another of similar prestige) rather than *vertical* career mobility (from one superintendency to another of higher prestige).[16] It appears that for the superintendent, the American dream of starting at the bottom (a small superintendency) and working to the top (a large superintendency) is just that; and only the exceptions realize the dream. Men at the top of the prestige hierarchy of the occupation ordinarily start near the top, and men who start near the bottom ordinarily stay near the bottom.

Several potential explanations of this seemingly unusual pattern present themselves as one views the occupation: the profit-loss measure, so common in business, is totally lacking in education, thus making it difficult for a superintendent to document in a readily acceptable fashion his success or failure; the position clearly seems to be one

---

[16] Regarding the extent of horizontal career mobility among superintendents see Earl E. Mosier and John E. Baker, "Midwest Superintendents on the Move," *Nation's Schools*, Vol. 49 (January, 1952), 44–46; Francis S. Chase and Robert E. Sweitzer, "Swiftly Come and Swiftly Go," *Nation's Schools*, Vol. 51 (March, 1953), 55–58; and James T. Castleberry, "The Turnover of Public School Superintendents in Arkansas" (Ph.D., diss., University of Arkansas, 1964).

from which no man can emerge without some blemishes on his record; a standard conversation among school superintendents revolves around the uniqueness of their school system, suggesting that experience is neither cumulative nor readily transferable; and in as much as the necessary qualities and skills demanded by the position are at best very vaguely articulated, it is difficult to understand how experience might significantly contribute.

DEMOGRAPHIC CHARACTERISTICS

School superintendents in the United States are drawn almost solely from the Caucasion race. The female superintendent is virtually extinct. Thus, it is very much a white male's occupation.[17]

Those who occupy the position tend to come from large families. A national survey of superintendents indicated that the mean number of children in the family was 4.5.[18] Goldberg reports that white women married from 1900 to 1909 (the time period in which the mean birth date of the sample members fell) had a mean of 3.9 children.[19]

Besides coming from large families, school superintendents over-represent the first born in terms of sibling order.[20] The significance of order of birth has been a subject of some interest to psychologists and psychoanalysts. Adler, for example, has asserted that there is a marked tendency towards conservatism among oldest children, that they revere the past, and are pessimistic about the future. Further, he indicates a belief that oldest children find pleasure in the exercise of authority and attach undue importance to rules and laws.[21]

---

[17] Data gathered in the mid-1950's in Massachusetts indicate that both superintendents and school boards felt that superintendents should be white males. Among the 105 superintendents sampled, 88 per cent felt that their replacement should be white, and no superintendent thought his replacement should be Negro. The school board members expressed similar feelings. Regarding sex, 95 per cent of the superintendents felt that their replacement should be male, while less than 1 per cent of the men thought the replacement should be female. See Gross, *Explorations in Role Analysis*, pp. 336, 338.

[18] AASA, *Profile of the School Superintendent*, p. 72.

[19] David Goldberg, "Fertility and Fertility Differentials: Some Observations on Recent Changes in the United States," in M. C. Sheps and J. C. Ridley, *Public Health and Population Change* (Pittsburgh: University of Pittsburgh Press, 1965), p. 122.

[20] Tables 2 and 3 in AASA, *Profile of the School Superintendent,* show the observed probability of being first born in the sample to be .316 and the expected probability was calculated to be .266. The difference between the probabilities yields a z value of 3.20 which has a p of .0014.

[21] H. L. Ansbacher and R. R. Ansbacher (eds.), *The Individual Psychology of Alfred Adler* (New York: Basic Books, Inc., Publishers, 1956), pp. 378–79.

The notion that first-born children are more likely to accept the values of the adult community is an oft-repeated assertion. Moreover, it has been demonstrated empirically that "regardless of social origins, family size, or the existence of an older brother, middle children have less successful careers than the first-born and the last-born. . . . The chief advantage enjoyed by men born either first or last, as well as by only children, is their better education." [22]

Size of Home Town

The various occupations do not draw randomly from the population as it is grouped according to size of place. Few large-city dwellers turn to farming as an occupation, and few farm-reared boys embark on careers as professional boxers. [23] A survey, taken in 1958 and published in the AASA *Profile of the School Superintendent,* asked the men to indicate the size of the community where they resided when they graduated from high school. [24] The mean age of the men in the sample was 51.8, indicating that the mean birth date was around 1906 and the mean age of the subjects at the time of the 1920 census was about 14. Table 2–3 shows the percentages of superintendents in relation to the percentages of the United States population residing in various sized places, and a ratio of the percentage of superintendents to the percentage of the population. The table indicates that school superintendents underrepresented the largest cities and overrepresented the smallest towns, but were in rather close approximation to the population from rural areas. Lack of data hinders exact comparisons with other occupational groups. However, the available data on the other occupations strikingly contrast with that on superintendents. Table 2–4 includes such data, which relate to American federal executives and business and military leaders. While the groupings under size of place in Tables 2–3 and 2–4 prevent precise comparison, the trends in the two tables are opposite. All of the occupational groups listed in Table 2–4 overrepresent the larger cities, while the superintendency underrepresents the large cities.

A more comprehensive view of the extent to which school superintendents overrepresent the population from small towns is afforded from data on college graduates. Table 2–5 compares data on size of

---

[22] Peter M. Blau and Otis Dudley Duncan, *The American Occupational Structure* (New York: John Wiley & Sons, Inc., 1967), p. 307.

[23] See S. Kirson Weinberg and Henry Arond, "The Occupational Culture of the Boxer," *American Journal of Sociology,* Vol. 57 (March, 1952), 460.

[24] *Loc. cit.,* p. 74.

Table 2-3

RESIDENCE OF SUPERINTENDENTS AT TIME OF HIGH SCHOOL GRADUATION

Size of Place	Percentage of Population (1920 Census)	Percentage of Superintendents	Ratio of Percentage of Superintendents over Percentage of Population
500,000 or more	15.5	2.0	.13
100,000 to 500,000	10.5	4.7	.45
10,000 to 100,000	16.5	13.8	.84
5,000 to 10,000	4.7	14.3	3.04
2,500 to 5,000	4.1	16.8	4.09
Under 2,500	48.8	41.2	.84

Table 2-4

RATIO OF SIZE OF BIRTHPLACE OF COMMUNITY LEADERS AND SIZE OF COMMUNITY TO U.S. POPULATION [*]

SIZE OF COMMUNITY	CAREER CIVIL SERVICE EXECUTIVES	POLITICAL EXECUTIVES	FOREIGN-SERVICE EXECUTIVES	CIVILIAN FEDERAL EXECUTIVES	BUSINESS LEADERS	MILITARY EXECUTIVES
400,000 and over	1.82	2.09	2.18	1.91	2.36	1.27
100,000–400,000	1.38	1.63	1.50	1.50	1.75	1.25
25,000–100,000	1.38	1.50	1.63	1.50	1.71	1.88
2,500–25,000	1.40	1.33	1.53	1.40	1.57	1.87
Under 2,500	0.64	0.55	0.48	0.59	0.43	0.57

[*] 1952 business leaders/1900 U.S. population = ratio; 1959 federal executives/1910 U.S. population = ratio

Source: W. Lloyd Warner, et al., *The American Federal Executive* (New Haven: Yale University Press, 1963), p. 58. Contrary to the data shown here about military executives Janowitz has stated, "The data on the place of birth of military leaders indicates that they are overwhelmingly of rural and small town origin." The difference might be in the sample. Warner included captains in the Navy and Colonels in the Army, Air Force, and Marine Corps, while Janowitz defined his elite as consisting only of those with a rank of Admiral or General. See Morris Janowitz, *The Professional Soldier* (New York: The Free Press, 1960), p. 86.

place of residence at time of graduation from high school from those 1961 college graduates who designated education as a career field with data from those who specified other careers. Although the table includes all who specified education as a career, school superintendents

Table 2–5

CORRELATION BETWEEN CAREER FIELD AND SIZE OF RESIDENCE
AT TIME OF HIGH SCHOOL GRADUATION
AMONG COLLEGE GRADUATES

CAREER FIELD	CORRELATION WITH LARGE CITY
Education	−.233
Physical Sciences	+.177
Biological Sciences	+.043
Social Sciences	+.307
Humanities	+.054
Medicine	+.211
Law	+.258
Engineering	+.051
Other Professions *	−.142
Business	+.138

* Other professions include dentistry, nursing, optometry, pharmacy, physical therapy, occupational therapy, veterinary medicine, medical technology, dental hygiene, "other health fields," agricultural sciences, forestry, fish and wild life management, farming, architecture, city planning, journalism, radio-television, communications, library science, theology and religion, public administration, foreign service, social work, home economics, military service.

Source: Table 5 is an adaptation of Table 2.3 in James A. Davis, *Undergraduate Career Decisions* (Chicago: Aldine Publishing Company, 1965), p. 11. The table is based on a representative sample of 33,982 June, 1961, graduates of colleges and universities.

are drawn heavily from this group. The table also reveals that education graduates are the least likely to come from large cities.

The comparisons, then, indicate that those in the school superintendency, in contrast to some other occupational fields, overrepresent the small town and rural population. Further, it appears that to a considerable extent, the educational establishment is the domain of the small town and rural person. All of this prompts the question "why?" Why are students from the small town and rural areas attracted to education and not other fields, and why are those from the larger cities not attracted to education?

In part, the answer seems to lie in the greater visibility of alternative occupations in cities. Youth in the towns and rural areas are exposed to fewer occupations than are youth of the cities. The young people in the towns and rural areas, however, are always exposed to education. Noting the greater social class and occupational mobility in cities as opposed to towns and rural areas, Bendix and Lipset account for the phenomena in part as follows:

> As well as having a better opportunity to obtain higher education, urban working-class youth are more likely to be acquainted with the occupational possibilities which exist in such communities than those who are raised in a less heterogeneous (occupationally) smaller community. In reanalyzing the occupational choices of school youth in a number of German and Austrian cities, Paul Lazarsfeld reported that "local variations in occupational choice are parallel to differences in economic structure." Thus, the larger the proportion of persons working in a particular kind of job in the city, the greater the number of 14-year-old school youths who desired to go into that occupation. Lazarsfeld interpreted this finding as follows: "The nature of occupational choice is not determined primarily as an individual decision, but rather is a result of external influences. For the occupational impressions offered by daily life are proportional to the actual occupational distribution. The greater the number of metal workers, the more frequently will young people hear about that occupation, and the greater will they be stimulated to choose it." [25]

Other authors, like Davis, find alternate explanations. Since those in the career field of education overrepresent the town and rural population, he wonders, "Does the difference come because big city public schools have a 'negative image,' because education is a relatively more visible occupation in smaller towns, because students from smaller cities are more likely to attend schools that stress teacher training, or because of other reasons?" [26]

Not only do school superintendents overrepresent the town and rural population, they also tend to exhibit limited geographical mobility. In either moving to the superintendency for the first time or moving from one superintendency to another, according to a national sample, slightly over 90 per cent of the moves are achieved without crossing state boundaries.[27] Moreover, Sharp reports that 79 per cent of the

---

[25] Seymour Martin Lipset and Reinhard Bendix, *Social Mobility in Industrial Society* (Los Angeles: University of California Press, 1963), pp. 220–21. Originally published by the University of California Press; reprinted by permission of The Regents of the University of California.

[26] James A. Davis, *Undergraduate Career Decisions* (Chicago: Aldine Publishing Company, 1965), p. 97.

[27] Snow and Hickcox, "Study of School Superintendents," Table 4.

school superintendents in Indiana work less than 100 miles from their birthplace and 26 per cent of them hold jobs within 25 miles of their birth sites.[28]

Noting the limited circulation of school superintendents and their predominantly town and rural background, which is unlike most college or university graduates, the career of the superintendent clearly does not depend on exposure to the occupational advantages of city dwellers or on high interest in geographical mobility.

Socio-Economic Class

Professional careers vary markedly in terms of ease of entry. Further, entry into a professional career is not equally easy for all men. The social class origin of entrants is related to the ease with which entry is gained to a professional career; a professional career is contingent on or conditioned by family status. In this section we will see the extent to which entry into the superintendency depends on social class. This calls for a comparison between the social class backgrounds of superintendents with those of other professionals.

First, it is acknowledged that those in the career field of education are drawn generally from the lower and middle social classes. Table 2–6 shows that those in the career field of education have the lowest socio-economic status of all career fields entered by other college or university graduates. The table shows correlations with high socio-economic status among a representative sample of 33,982 June, 1961, college and university graduates by career field.

Table 2–6 indicates that the career field of education is less strongly contingent on a high social-class background than is any other professional career. And although the table does not specifically concern itself with superintendents, it permits implications to be drawn about them. Because they are drawn from the field of education, the table implies that entry into the superintendency, like other occupations in the educational field, is not highly contingent on a high socio-economic background.

Father's occupation is reputed to have a high correlation with social class, and many consider it the best single predictor of social class. Further, those whose occupation is classified as professional stand at the top of the list; those in other occupational groups are lower down the

---

[28] Charles L. Sharp, "A Family, Experimental, and Educational Background Study of Superintendents of Schools in Indiana and Some Comparisons with Eleven other Midwest States" (Ph.D. diss., Indiana University, 1959), p. 34.

scale. Evidence indicates that only 11 per cent of the school superintendents had fathers whose occupations were classified as professional.[29]

Table 2–6

CORRELATION WITH HIGH SOCIO-ECONOMIC STATUS BY CAREER FIELD AMONG 1961 COLLEGE GRADUATES

CAREER FIELD	CORRELATION WITH HIGH SOCIO-ECONOMIC STATUS
Education	−.184
Physical Sciences	+.026
Biological Sciences	+.082
Social Sciences	+.215
Humanities	+.192
Medicine	+.370
Law	+.435
Engineering	−.120
Other Professions	000
Business	−.014

Source: An adaptation of Table 2.3 in James A. Davis, *Undergraduate Career Decisions* (Chicago: Aldine Publishing Company, 1965),

Table 2–7 indicates the extent to which this percentage conforms with or deviates from the percentage in other occupational groups. Note that school superintendents have the lowest percentage of fathers who were professionals. Perhaps the most meaningful comparison to be made is with all professional workers in the labor force. Here it can be seen that among the latter group 15.3 per cent had fathers who were employed in the professions, a percentage which is somewhat higher than that of superintendents.

It seems reasonable to conclude that in relative terms, entry into the superintendency has a very low dependency on the family's high socio-economic status.

Because superintendents come from small towns and rural areas and, therefore, lack the advantages of occupational mobility available

[29] Edward S. Hickcox, "Career and Place Bound Orientations of Chief School Officers in New York State: An Exploratory Study" (Ph.D. diss., Cornell University, 1966), p. 77.

Among a survey of all Oregon superintendents taken in the mid-1960's, 9.5 per cent had fathers who were professionals.

to the city dweller; because they, in comparison to other professional groups, come from lower socio-economic levels, and because fewer of their fathers were employed in the professions, it seems that through

Table 2-7

CORRELATION BETWEEN OCCUPATIONAL GROUPS AND PROFESSIONAL STATUS OF FATHERS

Occupational Groups	Percentage Whose Father's Occupation Classified as Professional
School superintendents [a]	11.0
D.D.S. students [b]	25.1
M.D. students [b]	31.1
American business elite [c]	14.0
High level civil servants [d]	28.3
U.S. Senators, 81st Congress, 1949–1951 [e]	22.0
U.S. Representatives, 77th Congress, 1941–1943 [e]	31.0
All professional workers [f]	15.3
33,982–1961 college graduates [g]	23.9
Military executives [h]	18.0

Sources: [a] Edward S. Hickcox, "Career and Place Bound Orientations of Chief School Officers in New York State: An Exploratory Study" (Ph.D. diss., Cornell University, 1966), p. 77.
   [b] Douglas M. More, "A Note on Occupational Origins of Health Service Professions," *American Sociological Review*, Vol. 25 (June, 1960), 404.
   [c] W. Lloyd Warner and James C. Abegglen, *Occupational Mobility in American Business and Industry* (Minneapolis: University of Minnesota Press, 1955), p. 40. Based on a 1952 study of 8,000 American business elite.
   [d] Reinhard Bendix, *Higher Civil Servants in American Society* (Boulder, Colo.: University of Colorado Press, 1949), p. 26.
   [e] Donald R. Mathews, *The Social Background of Political Decision Makers* (New York: Random House, 1954), p. 23.
   [f] Based on Bureau of the Census reports taken in 1962 as shown in Walter L. Slocum, *Occupational Careers* (Chicago: Aldine Publishing Company, 1966), pp. 166–67.
   [g] James A. Davis, *Undergraduate Career Decisions* (Chicago: Aldine Publishing Company, 1965), p. 207.
   [h] W. Lloyd Warner, *et al.*, *The American Federal Executives* (New Haven: Yale University Press, 1963), p. 346.

entry to the superintendency—a professional occupation—they are up-ward-mobile persons. The relatively low status of the superintendency suggests, however, that the climb is not extreme.

Education

Entry into a professional occupation depends on a requisite amount of formal education with a certain quality of academic performance. Standards relating to both amount and quality of performance vary among the professions. The states, rather than occupational peers, determine the standards for entry into the superintendency. The requirements generally include a bachelor's degree plus additional prescribed course work and evidence of "successful" teaching experience. The extent to which formal educational requirements constitute contingencies for entry into the superintendency is seen, in part, by a comparative view of the quality of the institutions of higher education attended by those in the various occupations. This view is given in Table 2–8, which shows the distribution of college graduates who majored in various career fields according to the quality ranking of institutions of higher education.

Table 2–8

UNDERGRADUATE MAJOR AND SCHOOL QUALITY

School Quality	Undergraduate Major (Percentages)								
	Edu-cation	Pre-Med	Social Sciences	Hu-man-ities	Physical Science	Engi-neer-ing	Bio-logical Science	Busi-ness	Other Pro-fessions
I–II	3	13	23	26	19	24	16	5	10
III	48	74	61	55	58	51	58	63	54
IV	49	13	16	20	23	26	26	31	36

Source: James A. Davis, *Undergraduate Career Decisions* (Chicago: Aldine Publishing Company, 1965), p. 249.

Table 2–8 shows that education majors attend the lowest-quality institutions. Only 3 per cent of the education majors attended institutions of the two highest-quality rankings, and 49 per cent of education majors attended institutions ranked last in the quality rankings. While the table does not deal specifically with superintendents, school superintendents generally are drawn from graduates who majored in education. Thus it seems reasonable to assume that they, too, receive their undergraduate education from institutions in the low-quality range. Hence entry into the superintendency apparently does not depend on ability to secure admission to and graduation from a high-quality institution of higher learning.[30]

---

[30] This is in marked contrast to the contingencies of the career as a Wall Street lawyer, where prestige or quality of the institution from which the law degree is gained is of prime importance. Among Wall Street lawyers, about 74 per cent graduated from Harvard, Yale, or Columbia law schools. See Erwin O. Smigel, *The Wall Street Lawyer* (New York: The Free Press, 1964), p. 39.

Although data do not exist on the academic performance of school superintendents, their records can be implied from the performance of college graduates designating education as a career field. Such persons, according to data assembled by Davis, have rather undistinguished records of academic performance. Among ten occupational career groups of college graduates (those cited in Table 2–8), the academic performance index of those in the career field of education is lower than seven of the groups and higher than two groups; it stands eighth out of ten in rank.[31] Apprehension about the low academic performance index (API) of those in education apparently caused Davis to add:

> Because there is considerable concern about education, it is important to put the findings on API in perspective. Although it is clear that lower academic achievement is associated with choice of education, we hope that the finding will not be seized out of context to forge an indictment. It is necessary to bear the following in mind: (1) Because of the large number of women in the field, education gets a reasonable cross-examination of API levels, the negative effect being only within sex. (2) Because four years of college represents considerable selection, there is no reason to believe that the bottom half of the college graduates are not academically strong enough to teach grade school and high school—if they have been trained in the appropriate content. (3) It is not clear that the very top students would be particularly good teachers, nor is it clear that the diversion of the academic elite from the arts and sciences and from medicine into education would serve the over-all interests of the nation. (4) The lack of an association with "original and creative" suggests that there is no selection on *anti*-intellectual values.
>
> None of this is to say that it is desirable to channel the dumbbells into education or that the intellectual level of the average faculty teaching education at the college level is outstanding. However, it should be noted that values and sex are much more important than API in recruitment to education; although the intellectual cream is clearly not opting for primary and secondary teaching, there is no evidence that the current situation spells intellectual disaster for future children.[32]

Assuming a high positive correlation exists between academic performance and intelligence, the next assumption is that, relative to other college graduates, those in education would not be distinguished by

---

[31] Davis, *Undergraduate Career Decisions*, p. 11.
[32] *Ibid.*, pp. 96–97.

high intelligence. This indeed seems to be the case. Wolfle reports that the mean intelligence score of those in education rates slightly below the mean of all college graduates and that the test scores place those in education seventeenth out of twenty college major fields. And among graduate students specializing in various fields, those in education rank fifteenth in a series of nineteen areas of specialization.[33] Furthermore, evidence indicates that male classroom teachers who drop out of the occupation have significantly higher intelligence than those who remain, and that male school administrators are not, in terms of intelligence, significantly different from those who remain as classroom teachers.[34]

Direct evidence about those doing graduate work in educational administration is provided by the norms of the Miller Analogies Test. Though it is not strictly an intelligence test, being constructed to predict success in graduate studies, the norms for the test indicate that among graduate students in seventeen fields attending universities which grant doctorate degrees, those in educational administration have the lowest mean score.[35]

As previously indicated, the formal educational requirements for the superintendency include a bachelor's degree plus graduate work varying from a few hours of credit to two years work beyond the bachelor's degree, depending on the regulations of the several states. Securing the formal graduate work required for the position seems to present relatively few hardships. The would-be superintendent ordinarily maintains full-time employment in a school system while undertaking the formal training. Unlike those in many professions, he need not remove himself from the gainfully employed while securing the required education. This arrangement is facilitated by university schools of education; they cater to the needs of their clients by making required course work available in the evening hours, on Saturday, and during the summer months when schools are closed. Moreover, school systems most often pay their certified employees according to the number of hours of college credit they have earned beyond the bach-

---

[33] See Dael L. Wolfle, *America's Resources of Specialized Talent* (New York: Harper and Brothers, 1954), pp. 199–200.

[34] See Robert L. Thorndike and Elizabeth Hagen, "Men Teachers and Ex-Teachers: Some Attitudes and Traits," *Teachers College Record*, Vol. 62 (January, 1961), 306–16. The evidence is based on a 1955 sample of 250 public school classroom teachers, 172 ex-classroom teachers, and 126 school administrators, primarily high school principals), all of whom had taken a common battery of tests in the Air Force in 1943.

[35] See W. S. Miller, *Miller Analogies Test Manual* (New York: The Psychological Corporation, 1960), pp. 6–7.

elor's degree. Thus, as the would-be superintendent is working away on credential requirements, he is also modestly increasing his salary by earning college credit. Further, it is only in the very sparsely populated states that he would need to travel more than one or two hours in order to reach some institution of higher education offering courses leading to the superintendent's credential. All things considered, securing the superintendent's credential is relatively painless.

In terms of amount of formal education, however, school superintendents seem to acquire and need for employment very little if any beyond that required for certification. Among a 1967 national sample of over 1,100 superintendents, only 13 per cent had acquired a doctorate degree. The vast majority, 83 per cent, reported a master's degree as their highest earned degree.[36]

In viewing education as a career contingency of the school superintendency, it is clear that formal and specialized training is necessary. However, it is equally clear that entry into the superintendency is not contingent on earning a college degree from a high quality school, achieving a better than average record of academic performance, having high intelligence in relation to other college graduates, or obtaining the greatest amount of formal education.

Marital Status

Entry into the superintendency and mobility within the occupation, however, are related to marriage. Simply being married enhances a school superintendent's career opportunities. Marriage, of course, has the opposite impact in some other occupations. As Polsky has pointed out, "Marriage is . . . a contingency that can adversely affect careers in many occupations . . . in [pool] hustling, much more frequently and intensely than in most occupations, marriage precipitates a genuine career crisis. . . . That is one reason why the great majority of career hustlers are career bachelors." [37]

Marriage is so crucial to the superintendency that editors of professional journals allocate space to many articles, written mainly by superintendents and/or their wives, which rehearse the role of the superintendent's wife and her importance to her husband's career. Among other things, it is reported that she should be ". . . cooperative, flexible, self-reliant . . . [and should] . . . bring well-bred social restraint to her relations with others in the community . . . [and that her] recog-

---

[36] Snow and Hickcox, "Study of School Superintendents," Table 5.

[37] Ned Polasky, *Hustlers, Beats and Others* (Garden City, N.Y.: Anchor Books, 1969), p. 74.

nition and understanding of the limitations of the status of school personnel is essential to good personal relationships . . ." [38]

Further, some data show that school superintendents and board members are opposed to superintendents who are either bachelors, widowers, or divorcees. Table 2–9 reveals these attitudes. One can infer from the data that the career of the superintendent depends on entry into the blissful state of matrimony and that the man should strive, in order to maximize his occupational opportunities, to keep his wife from separating herself from him by death or divorce. And it would appear that high school principals (the prime recruiting ground for superintendents), are exceptionally successful in keeping out of the divorce court; for, for example, the number of divorced among high school principals in Kentucky stands at respectable low of 1.5 per cent. [39]

Direct evidence about superintendents is available from a sampling, taken in the mid-1960s, of 84 of the 100 school superintendents in Oregon. All sample members were married and only two, or 2.4 per cent, of them had ever been divorced. Compared to expectations on the duration of marriage among the United States population, this percentage is noteworthy. The chances that a newly contracted marriage will end in divorce have been calculated and vary from 15.2 to 33 in 100, though not in a smooth curve, from 1922 to 1955. [40] Though these chance figures have been produced from data that included married persons who had previous divorces, among whom divorce is more common, [41] and though there is a slight chance (about 3 in 100 among the general population) [42] that some sample members, who on the average had been married over 25 years, will be divorced in the future, it is evident that the incident of divorce is from 6 to 14 times more common among the general population than it is among school superintendents. Further, divorce is related to occupation: among the

[38] Janne and Clyde Blocker, "The School Executive's Wife," *American School Board Journal,* Vol. 146 (May, 1963), 12.

[39] See Claude Frady, "The Principal in Profile," *Bulletin of the Bureau of School Service,* College of Education, University of Kentucky, Vol. 38, No. 3 (March, 1966), 13.

Though "divorced" is not parcelled out from "widowed or separated," it has been reported that among a national sample of elementary school principals, 9.5 per cent of all those ever married were either divorced, separated, or widowed. See Neal Gross and Robert E. Herriott, *Staff Leadership in Public Schools* (New York: John Wiley & Sons, Inc., 1965), p. 75.

[40] See Paul H. Jacobson, *American Marriage and Divorce* (New York: Rinehart & Co., Inc., 1959), p. 148; and Clifford Kirkpatrick, *The Family as Process and Institution* (New York: The Ronald Press, 1963), p. 591.

[41] Thomas P. Monahan, "The Changing Nature and Instability of Remarriages," *Eugenics Quarterly,* Vol. 5 (March, 1958), 73–85.

[42] Jacobson, *American Marriage and Divorce,* p. 145.

Table 2-9

ATTITUDES TOWARD MARITAL STATUS OF SUPERINTENDENTS

MARITAL STATUS	SUPERINTENDENTS [a] AND SCHOOL BOARD MEMBERS [b]					
	Per cent stating superintendent should be...		Per cent stating superintendent may or may not be...		Per cent stating superintendent should not be...	
	S	SB	S	SB	S	SB
Married	79	24	21	67	0	9
Married with children	52	39	48	61	0	0
Widower	0	0	70	81	30	9
Bachelor	0	1	43	75	57	24
Divorced	0	1	41	57	59	42

[a] n = 105
[b] n = 508

*Source: From an appendix table in Neal Gross, *et al.*, *Explorations in Role Analysis* (New York: John Wiley & Sons, Inc., 1958), pp. 335–38. By permission of John Wiley & Sons, Inc.

standard occupational classifications, divorce is least common among those in the professions.[43] Even when compared to the relatively low rate in the professions, the divorce rate among school superintendents is low. Weeks reports, from data gathered about 30 years ago, 6.8 divorces per 100 professionals.[44]

Religion

Affiliation with an organized religious body apparently has some connection with career of a school superintendent; both school board members and superintendents strongly feel that the latter should be "church members." Moreover, both groups feel that the superintendent should "take an active part in church affairs."[45] And among a national sample of superintendents, 75 per cent indicate they attend church weekly.[46]

School superintendents, as well as college graduates who designate education as a career field, overrepresent the Protestant and under-represent both the Catholics and Jews. The accompanying figure displays the extent to which the major religions are represented among college graduates who identify education as a career field as well as those specifying other career fields. Among the career fields represented, education attracts the second highest proportion of Protestants.

Among school superintendents, according to a national sample, 87 per cent cite Protestant as their religious preference.[47] This is considerably higher than the 62.4 per cent in the national population of white males who prefer the Protestant faiths.[48] Similarly, school superintendents claim the Protestant religions as preferred faith slightly more frequently than do United States Senators and substantially more frequently than do United States Representatives, even though both

[43] See William J. Goode, "Economic Factors and Marital Stability," *American Sociological Review*, Vol. 16 (December, 1951), 802–12.

[44] H. Ashley Weeks, "Differential Divorce Rates by Occupations," *Social Forces*, Vol. 21 (March, 1943), 334–37.

[45] See Gross, *Exploration in Role Analysis*, pp. 335, 339. Among a large sample of superintendents and board members in Massachusetts, 69 per cent of the superintendents and 75 per cent of the board members felt that superintendents should be "church members" and 63 per cent of the superintendents and 55 per cent of the board members felt that they should "take an active part in church affairs."

[46] See M. Kent Jennings and Harmon Zeigler, *"The Governing of School Districts* (Eugene, Ore.: Center for the Advanced Study of Educational Administration, University of Oregon, 1969), p. 3.

[47] *Ibid.*, p. 3.
Among Oregon superintendents, 90 per cent are Protestant.

[48] See U.S. Bureau of the Census, *Statistical Abstract of the United States* (1969), p. 41.

senators and representatives overrepresent the Protestant bodies.[49] And the proportion of school superintendents who are Protestant is nearly

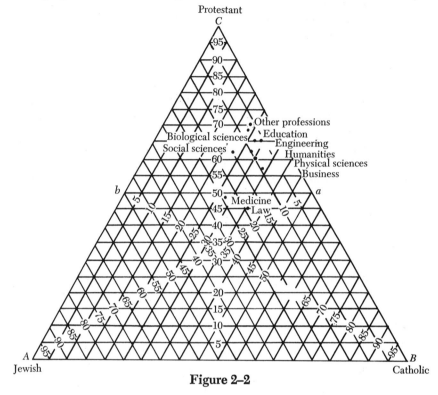

Figure 2–2

CAREER FIELD AND RELIGIOUS PREFERENCE

Source: James A. Davis, *Undergraduate Career Decisions* (Chicago: Aldine Publishing Company, 1965), p. 71.

equal to the proportion of the military elite—admirals and generals—who are Protestant.[50] As to which Protestant Church is most attractive

---

[49] See Donald R. Matthews, *The Social Background of Political Decision-Makers* (New York: Random House, 1954), p. 27.

[50] See Morris Janowitz, *The Professional Soldier* (New York: The Free Press, 1960), p. 98. Of the military elite in 1950, from 84 to 90 per cent were Protestant, depending on the branch of service, with the Air Force elite containing the fewest Protestants. Janowitz reports, on the other hand, that the percentage of Protestants in the West Point classes of 1959–60–61 ranged from 63 to 67. These lower percentages might signal a change in the composition of the future military elite or they might stand as evidence of the extent to which assent to the elite is contingent upon religious affiliation. Janowitz chose to say that "future trends are indicated from the West Point cadet classes of 1959, 1960, and 1961." (p. 97).

to school superintendents, the evidence indicates that the Methodist Church is the most frequently favored:[51] it is preferred by 42.5 per cent of the superintendents,[52] while it claims 13 per cent of the national population of white males.[53]

The overrepresentation of the Protestant religious bodies by school superintendents seems to be explained by several factors. Coming as they do from the small towns and rural areas, marked affiliation with the Protestant faiths should be expected because it is in these places that the Protestant churches are the strongest. Similarly, the fact that the Catholics operate elementary and secondary schools undoubtedly bears on the issue. Aside from these factors, it can be seen that school board members, the legal employers in public schools, are likewise overrepresentative of the Protestant bodies; 85 per cent of the board members serving in a representative national sample of school districts are reported to prefer the Protestant churches.[54]

Moreover, there is some evidence that school board members give preferential treatment to Protestant job applicants. The Cooks developed an employability index fo those with specified attributes and traits potentially seeking employment as classroom teacher. The index asked raters to assume that each "applicant" (as indicated in Table 2–10) was well-trained, certified, and qualified to teach, and, further, that an opening existed. The raters were then asked if those people would be employed in their schools. Subtracting the "yes" from the "no" replies, or vice versa, produced a positive or negative index number. Table 2–10, showing the index, permits comparisons among several groups. School board members clearly favor Protestants over Catholics or Jews among potential applicants for classroom teaching positions. It can thus be implied that school board members would also favor Protestants over Catholics or Jews among applicants for the superintendency.

Direct evidence of the extent to which school boards prefer Protestant superintendents is available from a sample of 508 Massachusetts school board members. The sample members were asked to assume they

---

[51] Comparative information about the characteristic of those of the Methodist religion is reported by Liston Pope, "Religion and the Class Structure," in Reinhard Bendix and Seymour Martin Lipset (ed.), *Class, Status and Power* (New York: The Free Press, 1953), pp. 316–23.

[52] Based on raw data from the survey by Jennings and Zeigler, *Governing of School Districts.*

[53] See Bureau of the Census, *Statistical Abstract of the United States* (1969), p. 41.

[54] See Jennings and Zeigler, *Governing of School Districts,* p. 3.

needed to replace their superintendents and to record their preferences among a number of attributes, including religious affiliation. Nine per cent of the sample thought the superintendent should be Protestant, while only one person in the sample thought he should not be Protestant. One member of the sample thought the man should be Catholic,

Table 2–10

EMPLOYABILITY QUOTIENT OF POTENTIAL APPLICANTS FOR TEACHING POSITIONS IN PUBLIC SCHOOLS

APPLICANT	As rated by			
	356 BOARD MEMBERS	2,095 LAY PERSONS	9,122 TEACHERS	3,054 STUDENTS
1. A known Protestant	76.5	84.9	93.5	93.5
2. Native-born, foreign name	56.3	73.2	88.5	89.9
3. Non-local resident	48.3	46.0	78.4	89.1
4. City-raised person	45.8	66.6	85.4	90.8
5. Out-of-state resident	15.4	27.5	69.4	64.9
6. A known Catholic	−21.3	9.5	53.1	68.0
7. A known pacifist	−22.8	5.3	29.7	40.4
8. A married woman	−32.1	−12.0	36.5	12.4
9. A known Jew	−41.3	2.3	44.8	41.5
10. A known militarist	−62.0	−50.1	−42.1	−25.0
11. A light Negro	−82.1	−54.2	−54.7	−33.6
12. A dark Negro	−85.7	−66.0	−63.4	−49.4
13. A known radical	−88.0	−72.5	−63.6	−48.2
14. Person in bad health	−93.3	−87.9	−54.7	−89.6
15. A known communist	−94.1	−83.2	−77.5	−57.9

Source: Lloyd Allen Cook and Elaine Forsyth Cook, *A Sociological Approach to Education* (New York: McGraw-Hill Book Company, 1950), p. 441.

while 9 per cent thought he should not be Catholic. And while no single member of the sample thought the replacement should be Jewish, 14 per cent thought he should not be Jewish.

The school superintendents employed by these school board members responded to the same items, but exhibited less neutral views about religious affiliation. Among them, 28 per cent thought their replacement should be Protestant, 20 per cent thought he should not be Catholic, and 35 per cent thought he should not be Jewish. No superintendent thought his replacement should not be Protestant, no one thought his replacement should be Jewish, and only 2 per cent thought he should be Catholic.[55]

Further evidence that entry into the superintendency is contingent on religious affiliation comes from noting the varying percentages of Protestant affiliation among teachers, school principals, and superintendents, as shown in Figure 2–3. Note that the higher the position in

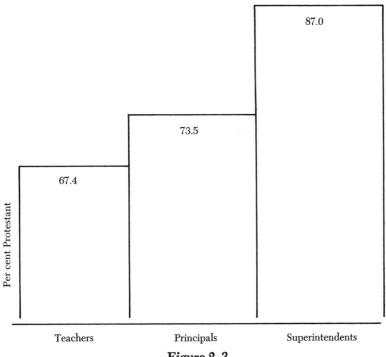

Figure 2–3

RELIGIOUS AFFILIATION AMONG TEACHERS, PRINCIPALS, AND SUPERINTENDENTS

Sources: ª Robert E. Herriott and Nancy Hoyt St. John, *Social Class and the Urban School* (New York: John Wiley & Sons, Inc., 1966), p. 121.
   ᵇ M. Kent Jennings and Harmon Zeigler, *The Governing of School Districts* (Eugene, Oreg.: Center for the Advanced Study of Educational Administration, University of Oregon, 1969), p. 3.

the school system hierarchy, the greater proportion of Protestants among the occupants. This can be interpreted to mean that religious affiliation has been an important contingency in movement up the public school authority structure and that opportunities for non-

---

[55] See Gross, *Explorations in Role Analysis,* pp. 337–38.

Protestants diminish progressively the higher the position in the hierarchy. Such an interpretation should be made with some caution for it would rest on the assumption that motivation to enter administrative posts is equally distributed among those of the various religious faiths. Also, the data on teachers and principals were taken from personnel in 187 elementary schools in 41 United States cities of over 50,000 population, while the data on superintendents came from a national sample of school districts representative of the public school student population; such juxtaposition of the two different samples might or might not depict a spurious picture.

Political Party Affiliation

School superintendents do not identify with the two major political parties in proportion to the distribution of the general population. A 1967 Gallup Poll reported political party identification in the general population to be 27 per cent Republican, 42 per cent Democrat, and 31 per cent independent. In the same year a national representative sample of superintendents revealed political party identification to be 45 per cent Republican, 34 per cent Democrat, and 20 per cent independent.[56] Another national survey, representative of the student population, showed the superintendents in those districts also to favor the Republican Party: among that group of men, 37 per cent were Republican, 28 per cent, Democrat, and 35 per cent, independent.[57] Thus school superintendents clearly overrepresent the Republican Party and underrepresent the Democratic Party. School board members likewise overrepresent the Republican Party and underrepresent the Democratic Party.[58] Moreover, attitudes of superintendents and board members show a preference for superintendents who are Republican.[59]

Political party identification is by no means a direct indicator of political beliefs or the content of such beliefs. Nevertheless, party identification at the present time must stand alone to speak for the political

---

[56] See Snow and Hickcox, "Study of School Superintendents."

[57] See Jennings and Zeigler, *Governing of School Districts*, p. 3.

[58] Garmire reported the breakdown of party affiliation among a sample of school board members in Oregon as 64 per cent Republican, 24 per cent Democrat and 12 per cent independent. See Leonard Garmire, "A Study of the Attitudes of School Board Members as They Relate to the Reasons for Seeking Office," *Oregon School Study Council Bulletin*, Vol. 6, No. 2 (Eugene, Oreg.: The School of Education, University of Oregon, 1962), p. 7. Jennings and Zeigler, *Governing of School .Districts*, p. 3, show political party affiliation of board members as 44 per cent Republican, 40 per cent Democrat, and 16 per cent independent.

[59] See Gross, *Explorations in Role Analysis*, pp. 335, 338.

beliefs of school superintendents. Those concerned with political beliefs have largely ignored education in general and school superintendents specifically, and those concerned with education have ignored political beliefs of those in the career field.[60] In part this might be attributable to the cultural dictum that schools should be kept out of politics, a dictum that Stephen K. Bailey labels "one of the most fascinating political items of American history."[61]

THE SUPERINTENDENCY: AN OPEN ELITE

The term *elite* refers to those with the greatest amount of power or potential power: the final decision makers. Within any profession a small group of men can be thought of as constituting the elite. In the vast arena of public elementary and secondary schools, the school superintendents can be thought of as constituting the elite—they hold the most power; they are the final decision makers (though their power is being whittled down by teachers' organizations).

The character of informal and formal requirements for elite status varies widely among the professions and the standards are set at differing levels. Thus, in a sense, elites can be viewed as being relatively open or closed in the several professions; entry into the elite can be seen as relatively easy or relatively difficult.

The material on the career contingencies of the superintendency detailed in this chapter seems to support the judgment that the superintendency constitutes a relatively open elite. The barriers for entry into the occupation seem to be few. Family background seems to present few obstacles: the superintendents come from the small towns and rural areas, and from large lower and middle-class families; relatively few of their fathers were professionals. Though formal educational requirements exist, they do not seem to present a real challenge or to restrict entry seriously. Most school superintendents obtain less than the full amount of formal education available; and there is no reason to believe that they possess distinguished academic records, that they took their basic college education at institutions of distinction, or that they possess relatively outstanding basic intelligence. All of this is not

[60] After examining the evidence from a number of studies, Goldhammer suggests that "the conclusion that school board members are predominantly politically conservative cannot be contested." This being the case it does not seem unreasonable to assume that those hired by school boards, superintendents, would also be politically conservative. See Keith Goldhammer, *The School Board* (New York: The Center for Applied Research in Education, Inc., 1964), p. 97.

[61] Stephen K. Bailey, *et al.*, *Schoolmen and Politics* (Syracuse, N.Y.: Syracuse University Press, 1962), p. viii.

to say that school superintendents have no ability, skill, or basic competence. The point is, relatively speaking, the superintendency seems to be an open elite.

However, the superintendency is not without barriers. And although there is not a mass of data about all potential barriers, it appears that religion, political party affiliation, and marital status all play a part in entry into and movement through the occupation. It has been shown that superintendents overrepresent the Protestant faiths and the Republican Party, and the attitudes of superintendents and school board members show a bias against divorcees, widowers, or bachelors occupying the superintendency.

Although the school superintendents can be thought of as constituting the elite of public elementary and secondary education, there are many elite groups. An elite group exists in every profession or occupational group and in perhaps every field of endeavor. All of these functional elites are combed, sorted, and sifted; and some individuals are selected for entry in *Who's Who in America,* the nationally recognized listing of the leading men and women in contemporary American life. In this master listing of the prominent citizens of the land, how do those who manage the public schools fare? The occupants of many positions or statuses automatically qualify for listing (Senator, some Judges, etc.) but holding a school superintendency does not qualify one for automatic listing; and, therefore, the superintendents must win their place in open competition.

School superintendents do not command much space in *Who's Who.* A 10 per cent random sample of all school superintendents listed in the 1966 *Roster* of American Association of School Administrators was checked with the 1966–67 *Who's Who* and the results indicate that about 0.43 per cent of the superintendents [62] or about 4 in 1,000 are listed in *Who's Who.* [63]

No listing of the prominent pleases all or suits all needs; thus, in addition to *Who's Who,* a listing of the *functional elite,* there is the *Social Register,* a listing of the *social elite.* [64] But school superintendents are

---

[62] Not all superintendents are members of the American Association of School Administrators. Those earning low salaries, having relatively limited formal education, and employed in the smaller school systems tend not to join the Association. Thus this percentage is probably inflated due to the source of the sample.

[63] Among the superintendents in the twenty largest cities in the United States, 55 per cent were listed in *Who's Who.*

[64] In cities where the *Social Register* exists there is considerable overlap between listings in it and *Who's Who.* "Of the 12,530 residents of these twelve metropolitan areas which have a *Social Register* who were listed in *Who's Who . . .* 23 per cent were also listed in the *Social Register.*" E. Digby Baltzell, *Philadelphia Gentlemen* (New York: The Free Press, 1966), p. 29.

not to be found in listings of the socially prominent: no school super-intendent of the central city in some twelve metropolitan areas for which the *Social Register* exists was listed.[65] Both *Who's Who* and the *Social Register* listings are national in scope though the *Social Register* is far less so than *Who's Who*. At the local level there has been con-siderable activity by scholars seeking to identify the power elite in the local community. The numerous studies have consistently documented the absence of school superintendents from those who constitute the community power elite.[66]

"Easy come, easy go" seems to be a folk saying with relevance to the superintendency. It appears to be a relatively open elite, one for which entry is relatively easy. But it also appears to be one elite from which many exit.[67]

---

[65] Thirty per cent of the partners of Wall Street law firms are listed in the New York *Social Register*. See Smigel, *The Wall Street Lawyers*, p. 39.

[66] See Ralph B. Kimbrough, *Political Power and Educational Decision-Making* (Chicago: Rand McNally & Co., 1964), pp. 30, 50, 80, 90–100.

[67] See John F. Cramer, "What Happens to City Superintendents in Oregon?" *School Executive*, Vol. 70 (1951), 54–55; Wesley C. Meierhenry, "The Subsequent Careers of 524 Men Who Were Administrators in 1930–31" (M.A. thesis, Uni-versity of Nebraska, 1941); and Donald Hair, *Tenure and Turnover of Wyoming Public School Superintendents* (Laramie, Wyo.: Curriculum and Research Center, College of Education, University of Wyoming, 1956). Cramer reports that, during a 30 year period, 20 per cent of the superintendents of First Class districts in Oregon left the superintendency and education for other fields. Meierhenry reports the percentage to be 32 and Hair indicated 11 per cent for his sample. A con-temporary sampling of Oregon superintendents indicates that slightly more than one out of six do not wish to remain in the occupation until retirement.

3

Successors: Career-Bound and Place-Bound

School superintendents, with few exceptions, rise from the ranks of those employed in public schools. To hold a super-intendency, a man must have a state-awarded credential. For the credential, the potential superintendent usually must provide evidence of some successful experience as a classroom teacher and present a specified number and type of university credits. By the time the requirements are met, most individuals have gained administrative experience in some position like a school principalship. Ultimately, two courses of action are open to the would-be superintendent: one is to wait until the superintendency comes to him, and the other is to seek a superintendency wherever it can be found.

PLACE-BOUND AND CAREER-BOUND SUPERINTENDENTS

The man who waits simply continues work in the home school system until the superintendency is his. He may wait in vain; nevertheless, he waits. His career is an ascent through the hierarchy in one school system, although he may have changed school systems earlier at some level beneath the superintendency. He is usually older than the man who does not wait when he takes office as superintendent. The man who waits is promoted to the superintendency from within and has held one or more positions in the system immediately before becoming its superintendent. Ordinarily he completes his career as superintendent in the home system and thus is a one-city superintendent. If he leaves the superintendency before retirement age, he often takes a newly created lower-level administrative position in the same home district.

The man who does not wait is promoted to the superintendency from outside. His career is always spread over two or more school systems. Having been brought in from outside, he has never served his new district in any capacity other than as superintendent. Ordinarily his career does not stop with one superintendency. To a greater extent than the man who has been promoted from within, he makes a career as superintendent rather than as a public-school employee.

There is a motivational distinction between superintendents who arrive at the position by way of promotion from within and those who arrive at the position by way of promotion from outside, a distinction in the importance they assign to career and location. Both have made investments and sacrifices to obtain the superintendent's credential. The man promoted from within, however, seems to want to career as superintendent only if he can have it in his home school system. He puts place of employment above a career as superintendent.[1] Superintendents promoted from within are called *place-bound*.

The man promoted from outside puts career above place. He leaves the home school system and takes a superintendency elsewhere. He is bound not to a place, but to a career. Superintendents advanced to the

---

[1] Maurice D. Adams makes some instructive comments about attachment to the home community on the part of candidates for the superintendency. Adams, according to his message, was seeking the superintendency in this home community, but the school board was debating whether or not to fill the vacant position from within. At the request of the board, he submitted to them a letter assessing arguments for and against promotion from within. Writing in the letter about his formal education he said ". . . throughout my training in administration, I have had the X system in mind and practically everything I have learned has been learned in its relation to our own needs and problems here. That has been my great motivator." Lamenting the possibility that the position would not be filled from within, he regretted being forced to the conclusion that ". . . the only way for an able man to advance is to leave his own community. . ." And the importance of place of employment he summed up as follows. ". . . If the superintendency is important, it is still more important that the superintendent look upon his community as his home rather than the temporary place of his employment." Adams did not get the job; he moved from the community—not, however, into a superintendency. See "Promotion from Within or Without?" *The American School Board Journal*, Vol. 130 (May, 1955), 63, 104.

superintendency from outside the containing organization are called *career-bound.*

These two categories have not been inferred from written answers to a questionnaire or from spoken responses in interviews. Superintendents place themselves in these categories through their actions. The route one follows to the superintendency, or more precisely, the origin of the man in relation to the containing organization, determines his placement in the categorical scheme.

SOURCES OF MOTIVATION AND ACTION

To wait for the superintendency or to seek it is a major decision in an individual's career. Many factors are involved. The man who waits commits himself in a way that differs from that of the man who does not wait.[2]

The terms *place-bound* and *career-bound* are meant to convey two important distinctions in the latent roles of the two types. (*Latent* describes a role or commitment that is not officially or normally a part of the position. It may be inactive or fully activated, but at least it has the potential of shaping the performance in the position. For example, during a community disaster a volunteer fireman, because of his latent role as a household head, might go home rather than to the fire station. If a school teacher systematically exploits her student by tutoring on a fee basis, her latent role of privately employed tutor is shaping action in the manifest role of publically employed teacher.[3]). The first distinction meant to be conveyed by categorization has been suggested above by pointing out that the place-bound superintendent is more

---

[2] Several researchers have gathered data on personality characteristics of categories of individuals having commitments similar to those of place-bound and career-bound superintendents. Marvick has written about "institutionalists" and "specialists" in a federal agency. Some differences between "locals" and "cosmopolitans" on a college faculty have been pointed to by Gouldner. And Avery has massed data on potential "passive" and "active managers." There seems to be a likeness among institutionalists, locals, passive managers, and inside superintendents as well as among specialists, cosmopolitans, active managers, and outside superintendents. See Dwaine Marvick, *Career Prospectives in a Bureaucratic Setting,* Michigan Government Studies No. 27 (Ann Arbor: University of Michigan Press, 1954); Alvin W. Gouldner, "Cosmpolitans and Locals: Toward an Analysis of Latent Social Roles—I and II," *Administrative Science Quarterly,* Vol. 2 (December, 1957), 281–306, and Vol. 2 (March, 1958), 444–480; and Robert W. Avery, "Orientation Toward Careers in Business: A Study in Occupational Sociology," (Ph.D. diss., Harvard University, 1959).

[3] For an extended definition of latent role see Gouldner, "Cosmopolitans and Locals," Part I.

interested in place than career and that the opposite is true for the career-bound superintendent. The place-bound superintendent, who places high value on residing in a specific community, wishes to continue receiving the rewards of long-time community residence. On the other hand, the career-bound superintendent places greater value on a career as superintendent than on life in a specific community.

The second distinction is that the place-bound superintendent has a history in the school system and, thus, has an established part in the organization's informal operations and activities. His ties, commitments, friends, enemies, and obligations are known. Career-bound superintendents, however, do not have a history in the school system. They are "strangers" in the sociological sense of the word.

The fact that the place-bound superintendent has a history in the social organization of the school system and that the career-bound superintendent does not should not be viewed lightly. It might have significance for organizational effectiveness. Various team studies demonstrate that two characteristics of leaders are crucial for team effectiveness. One is that the leader must be acceptable to his followers; and, as Michels has observed:

> Among the party leaders will be found men who have acquired fame solely within the ranks of the party, at the price of long and arduous struggles, but the masses have always instinctively preferred to these those who have joined them when already full of honor and glory and possessing independent claims to immortality. Such fame won in other fields seems to them of greater value than that which is won under their own eyes.[4]

The second characteristic important for our purposes is that the leader must maintain a phychological distance between himself and his followers.[5] Because of his history in the organization, the place-bound superintendent seems less likely than the career-bound superintendent to be able to maintain the amount of psychological distance from his subordinates necessary for effective organizational performance. Further, it can be argued on the grounds of past research that the place-bound superintendent is more likely to conform to the wishes of his subordinates than is the career-bound superintendent. Probably the most recent reference point of the man promoted from within is

---

[4] Robert Michels, *Political Parties: A Sociological Study of the Oligarchical Tendencies of Modern Democracies* (New York: The Crowell-Collier Publishing Company, 1962), pp. 101–2.

[5] See Fred E. Fiedler, *Leader Attitudes and Group Effectiveness* (Urbana, Ill.: University of Illinois Press, 1958), chapter IV.

that of the man second in command. He probably has held such a position a few years before his succession. Small-group research indicates that people second in command will more likely conform to the judgment of others than people first or last in command.[6] It seems reasonable to assume that whatever made the second in command more influenced by others could not or would not be readily unlearned, and that this pattern would carry over when the second in command moved to the top position within the same group.

Much of the pattern of action used by successors in relating to an organization is predictable and understandable because the place-bound superintendent has a high commitment to a specific community, a low commitment to a career as superintendent, and a history in the social system of the school district; the career-bound superintendent, on the other hand, lacks a commitment to life in a specific community, has a high commitment to a career as superintendent, and lacks a history in the social system of the school district.

Types of Career-Bound Superintendents

Within the category of career-bound superintendents there are three discernible subtypes: *hoppers, specialists,* and *statesmen.*[7] The classification does not imply, however, that all career-bound superintendents fit one of these subtypes. There is a residual category. Hoppers earn their name from frequent moves from one school district to another. In addition to these moves, hoppers have at least two other characteristics. First, their movements do not take them to larger districts. Each move is to a district similar to the one before. And second, hoppers always have an application out; they are always seeking a new superintendency. The way they relate to the school system while superintendent and some of their motives for moving are apparent in the comments of three superintendents.

---

[6] In this connection it is important to note the results of a recent small group experiment by O. J. Harvey. Essentially the experiment presented stimuli to a group and to either the group's leader, second in command, or lowest ranking member and called for judgments about what was seen. The procedure was such that all thought they viewed the same stimuli but what was presented to the leader, or second in command, differed from what was presented to the group. The basic finding was that the second in command discounted his own judgments of what he saw and thus was more conforming to judgments of the group than either the leader or the lowest ranking person. See O. J. Harvey and C. Consalvi, "Status and Conformity to Pressures in Informal Groups," *Journal of Abnormal and Social Psychology,* Vol. 60 (1960), 182–87.

[7] Superintendents quite frequently used the term *hopper,* but the other two subtypes were usually unnamed in their descriptions.

He moves into a community and he's like a firecracker. He goes and he has done something. He has done something really worthwhile, but in the community he's led them too fast and they begin to back down on him a little bit and the first thing—he's a smart operator—he moves to the next hop—they'll move here and there and anywhere—but they keep moving. Now, they did something for the community but they did it too fast—but the next community looking at him says—'Well, he can do that and we're willing to take our chances on him. We'll grab him and go with him.'

He just likes to start things and doesn't like to stick it to the finish —to carry them through. He's usually a candidate and it satisfies something in his ego to be able to be accepted, even though it isn't anything of a promotion—here's another board that likes me—and that sort of thing.

Some of the boys jump from one state to the other. I recall one who came, well I believe he was in Connecticut, then he went to New York State, and then to Pennsylvania, and now he's out in Michigan. Now, some of the boys don't look with favor on that type of thing because in the first place he doesn't have any roots and some feel that he's just an opportunist that comes in, does a job, and leaves. Now, maybe he has a place in the field of education— I'm not sure. Well he came in very popular at first, but by the end of the term he was considered very unpopular, not only with the board but with his community. He seemed to have the ability to sell himself in a certain situation, but in other words, he didn't wear well. He made a good first impression but wasn't able to carry through over a period of time. This boy always moved far enough away that the local gossip didn't follow him too much.

A specialist makes a longer, more systematic commitment to a community. But like a hopper, a specialist must leave once his task has been accomplished. The specialist earns a reputation for doing some task very well; he gains his satisfaction from doing a specific job. He moves among small districts where the superintendent is the whole administrative force, in systems lacking the size to warrant specialists in subsuperintendent posts. Specialists concentrate in areas such as buildings, finance, curriculum, public relations, and personnel.

A school board takes on a specialist for a specific job. When it is well along or finished the board needs somebody else or the man looks for a place to start the same process all over again. The reputation the specialist builds is important to him because his future positions depend on it. The hopper, on the other hand, tries to explain away his reputation by saying that the community was not ready for him. The following comments made by three superintendents are instructive regarding specialists.

I know some superintendents who are devoted to their positions, not in any one community, who have felt that they have certain strong points—financial reorganization of a school district—to put it on a sound basis—so, they take a position in a school district—they'll work in a school district for maybe four years, five years, six years, until they feel that they have that school district in a good, sound, financial situation. Then they'll tour the highways—by watching the roadmap which they've laid out for the situation so that the school district keeps going on—and they'll start looking for someplace else where they can do the same type of a job.

.. There's also the man who's especially good in the field of education, in developing curriculum for a district while he may not be so good on a building program, and then, of course, there are others who are especially good in finance. That's the one that's usually called in after a building program to help solve the financial problems. There's a rule of thumb that if you do much building you'll be moving on. I don't mean that when we say superintendents fall in a certain category like a builder or a curriculum man that that's the only thing he can do. It's considered his strength and is usually well known.

I've known in certain instances where superintendents were hired primarily to carry out the job of the shake-up in the staff to get certain changes made and after those were made, he moved on to another district. . . . In the cases that I have in mind, they moved on by choice. While he's still popular, he moves.

The statesman's commitment to a community differs. He usually stays from four to ten years and during this time moves all phases of the educational program as far as he can; at that point, he considers other jobs. He takes pride in the fact he never is a candidate for a new superintendency; school boards come to him. Each time he moves he goes to a larger school system. He is careful, as is the specialist, about the impression he leaves behind, for his reputation is important. Because of his work quality and his concern for the long-range consequences of his acts for the whole educational program in the schools he serves, he is called a statesman.

DISTRIBUTION

Place-bound and career-bound superintendents exist in unequal numbers. A secondary analysis of raw data gathered for the American Association of School Administrators in a 1960 nationwide survey of school superintendents [8] indicates that of 859 sampled superintendents, about 35 per cent were place-bound and about 65 per cent were career-bound.[9] Another national survey of over 1,100 superintendents conducted in the mid-1960's reports a similar distribution: 31 per cent place-bound and 69 per cent career-bound.[10]

However, deviations from this distribution can be found. The Snow and Hickcox survey reports that 41 per cent of the superintendents in the East-Central region of the nation were promoted from within, as were 21 per cent of the superintendents in the Plains states. A more extreme deviation from the general distribution of the two types occurs in West Virginia. A sample of 46 of the 55 superintendents in the state taken in 1964 indicated that 85 per cent as opposed to the expected 35 per cent of the men had been promoted from within. Moreover, informants asserted that the 1964 cohort was not atypical.

The prevailing practice of promotion in West Virginia begs an explanation. What factors account for the overwhelming proportion of superintendents promoted from within? Or more generally, what factors influence the variation in the ratio of place- and career-bound superintendents in a given region or during a given time span? Here the ground is soft; data to support an explanation have not been collected, and what is advanced is merely a guess.

It seems reasonable to assume, though, that the degree of affluence would affect the ratio. Seemingly a strong argument could be advanced for promotion from within during a period of scarcity of money and jobs. After all, promotion from within awards the job to a member of the community, not to a stranger. Further, promotion from within frees a job, the job vacated by the new superintendent. Also, as will be shown in detail later, it costs less to fill a superintendency from within. Thus during a time of scarcity of money and jobs several factors recommend the practice of promotion from within.

In addition, cultural factors within the school system might influence the decision about the origin of the new superintendent. For examples, the religious commitments of the clients of the school system or the mix of ethnic or racial groups and the special history of the relationships might compel the employing board to avoid a man who

---

[8] The AASA's report of the data can be seen in *Profile of the School Superintendent* (Washington, D.C., 1960). The details of the sample are given on pages 4 and 71.

[9] For comparative data on origin of executives in big business see Mabel Newcomer, "The Big Business Executive," *Industrial Man*, W. L. Warner, *et al.* (ed.), (New York: Harper and Brothers, 1959), pp. 130ff.

[10] Snow and Hickcox, "Study of School Superintendents."

lacked understanding, understanding that could come only with long immersion in the situation. And finally, politics (in the negative sense) might play a part.

Along with the unequal number of career- and place-bound superintendents and the variation in their ratios from place to place, the two kinds of superintendents are unevenly distributed across school systems of varying sizes. Table 3–1 shows the distribution according to school district size.

Those promoted from within are overrepresented in the larger systems. About 17 per cent of all place-bound and only about 9 per cent of all career-bound superintendents work in systems of more than 100,000 inhabitants. And reading across, about 61 per cent of the superintendencies in cities over 500,000 and 46 per cent of the superintendencies in cities over 100,000 are held by place-bound men. Chance alone would indicate that all superintendencies in all size systems should be split on a 35/65 basis.

Over-all, the table indicates the tendency for larger school systems to promote to the superintendency from within. This suggests something about the availability of replacements from within and about the nature of the position. The tendency to promote from within contrasts with the earlier practice in the same large cities when the office of superintendent was first established.[11] The character of the office has changed since then. As some have argued, the men occupying the superintendency in the larger systems no longer are the elite; and in large systems, the office of the superintendent is not so important anymore. Large cities are not innovation leaders as they once were. Now the demands of the position in large cities place a heavy burden on public relations; thus men from inside, men who know the situation and are themselves known, can best hold the changed position.

---

[11] Theodore L. Reller made this observation in private conversation. For the historical background of the superintendency see his book, *The Development of the City Superintendency in the United States* (Philadelphia: privately published, 1935).

Table 3-1

DISTRIBUTION OF CAREER- AND PLACE-BOUND SUPERINTENDENTS

POPULATION OF SCHOOL DISTRICT	PLACE-BOUND			CAREER-BOUND		
	NUMBER	PERCENTAGE OF PLACE-BOUND SUPERINTENDENTS	PERCENTAGE OF POSITIONS IN POPULATION CLASS	NUMBER	PERCENTAGE OF CAREER-BOUND SUPERINTENDENTS	PERCENTAGE OF POSITIONS IN POPULATION CLASS
500,000 and over	11	4%	61%	7	1%	39%
100,000 to 499,999	38	13	46	44	8	54
30,000 to 99,999	68	24	44	88	17	56
10,000 to 29,999	85	29	32	177	33	68
5,000 to 9,999	65	22	31	145	27	69
2,500 to 4,999	22	8	23	72	14	77
Totals	289	100%	—	533	100%	—

Source: Secondary analysis of data contained in AASA, *Profile of the School Superintendent.*

4

Successors: Career Styles

Superintendents whose origins are from within the school
system have been labeled place-bound, and those whose origins are from outside the containing organization have been
called career-bound. These labels were selected to convey
a distinction between the two types in respect to the commitment they have to their career as a superintendent. In
that the man promoted from within waits in his home school
system for the superintendency to come to him and that the
man brought in from outside does not wait but seeks the
position, it can be inferred that the career-bound superintendent has a higher commitment to the superintendency
than does the place-bound superintendent. In this chapter
the implication is made concrete.

Strength of commitment is only one aspect of a career. As
an individual decides on a career, prepares for it, assumes it,
forms attitudes about it, and leaves a trace through a series
of jobs, he exhibits a career style. Besides examining the
career commitments of the two kinds of superintendents, an
attempt will be made here to portray central features of
their career styles.

Careers develop within channels created by the interplay
of aspirations, competencies, and perceived opportunities.

49

These factors reflect not only the past and the present, but also the future as imagined or estimated by the individual. The very decision to aspire to a given career is in itself of prime importance in shaping the eventual career. The decision to aspire focuses attention and excludes a heuristic approach. Some occupations require an early decision to seek entry because of the long training necessary. In other occupations one may delay the decision while gaining experience and playing out alternatives. The school superintendency as a career falls in the latter category. Most potential superintendents first commit themselves by training as a teacher. While thus engaged, and while in their early thirties, they formulate the aspiration for a superintendency.

Although the decision to aspire to the superintendency is made relatively late among most would-be superintendents, career- and place-bound superintendents do differ. The open-ended question, "Why did you enter the superintendency?" naturally elicites a variety of responses. Some, however, reflect the decision to aspire to the superintendency. Some responses indicate that the man decided to be a superintendent when the opportunity came. For example, "The job turned up and there I was." "Just happened that this [superintendency] turned up." "Had not given much thought to the position before this opportunity came up." Such comments were made by 1 per cent of the career-bound and 42 per cent of the place-bound superintendents. On the other hand, some responses showed that the superintendency was a long-standing ambition. Examples include "The superintendency becomes a normal goal once in education." "Always wanted to be superintendent, sort of my ambition." "Aimed from the first for it; planned jobs to get experience in all grades; I decided to be a superintendent when I decided to enter education." Such comments were made by 42 per cent of the career-bound and 24 per cent of the place-bound superintendents.[1]

Furthermore, when superintendents are asked to specify the age when they made the decision to aspire to the superintendency, career-bound men indicate a younger age. In a sample of 102 Massachusetts superintendents, the mean age for career-bound superintendents at the time this decision was made was 29, and the mean age for place-bound superintendents was 37.[2] Similarly, in a sample of 83 Oregon superintendents, the mean age was 30 for career-bound and 36 for place-bound superintendents.

---

[1] These data were obtained by a secondary analysis of data collected by Gross in *Explorations in Role Analysis*.
[2] *Ibid.*

Such age differences between the two types is reflected when appointed to their first superintendency. The mean age on assuming the first superintendency was 35.7 for career-bound and 44.3 for place-bound superintendents in a sample of 185 Oregon and Massachusetts superintendents.

These data, then, indicate that career-bound men commit themselves earlier to the superintendency than do place-bound men. One could argue, though perhaps not too convincingly, that early commitments have higher value to the individual than later commitments as far as careers are concerned. Logically, commitments made early and fulfilled later are stronger than those made and acted on almost simultaneously. The former is more descriptive of career-bound superintendents, and the latter is more descriptive of place-bound superintendents. Among a sample of 102 superintendents from Massachusetts and 83 from Oregon, 90 per cent of the career-bound men and 60 per cent of the place-bound men indicated a lapse of years between the time they decided to aspire to the superintendency and the time they assumed their first superintendency.

Thus when considering the basic decision to be a school superintendent, career-bound men make an earlier commitment to the superintendency as an occupation, enter the occupation at an earlier age, and commit themselves beforehand to a significantly greater extent than do place-bound superintendents.

PREPARATION FOR CAREER

While the decision to aspire to a given career is important in the ultimate career one traces out, the way and the extent to which one prepares himself for a career is also a matter of importance.

Career and place-bound superintendents also exhibit different patterns of preparation for the career. Career-bound men tend to complete their formal education beyond the bachelor's degree at a younger age than place-bound men.[3] Career-bound superintendents are also more likely to have attended a graduate school as a full-time student

---

[3] The Snow and Hickcox national survey of superintendents shows that among those whose highest degree was an M.S. or M.A., the mean time elapsed between the Bachelor's and Master's degree was eight years for career-bound and nine years for place-bound superintendents. Among those whose highest degree was a Ph.D. or an Ed.D., the mean time elapsed between the Bachelor's and Doctor's degree was fifteen years for career-bound and seventeen years for place-bound superintendents.

than place-bound superintendents.[4] Of greater import in terms of commitment to the career is the fact that career-bound superintendents obtain a greater amount of education, at least as measured by formal education, than do place-bound superintendents.

Table 4–1 shows the distribution of formal educational attainment for a group of 719 school superintendents. The sample includes 83 superintendents from Oregon; 61 from Allegheny County, Pennsylvania; 102 from Massachusetts,[5] and 473 from New York.[6] About 11 per cent of the place-bound superintendents and about 25 per cent of the career-bound superintendents obtain either an Ed.D. or Ph.D. The difference between the amount of education obtained by the two types of superintendents yields a chi-square of 18.5, significant at the .001 level of confidence.

Table 4–1

FORMAL EDUCATION OF SUPERINTENDENTS

	AMOUNT OF EDUCATION	
TYPE OF SUPERINTENDENT	Less than Ed.D. or Ph.D.	Ed.D. or Ph.D.
Place-Bound	236	30
Career-Bound	342	111

Source: Secondary analysis of data reported by Edward S. Hickcox, "Career and Place Bound Orientations of Chief School Officers in New York State: An Exploratory Study (Ph.D. diss., Cornell Universitiy, 1966), p. 64.

Not only do career-bound superintendents obtain a higher level of formal education, they also receive their education at institutions of higher prestige. The graduate schools of longest attendance by a sample of 473 New York State school superintendents were ranked according to prestige by a panel.[7] Table 4–2 shows that the mean prestige ranking

---

[4] Among a sample of 83 Oregon superintendents, data taken prior to the time when most schools of education initiated a residence requirement show that about 30 per cent of the career-bound and about 20 per cent of the place-bound superintendents were full-time graduate students during the regular academic year at some time during their graduate studies.

[5] Data obtained from secondary analysis of raw data collected by Gross for *Explorations in Role Analysis.*

[6] Data obtained from secondary analysis of data reported by Hickcox, "Career and Place Bound Orientations," p. 64.

[7] Data obtained from secondary analysis of data reported by Hickcox, "Career and Place Bound Orientations," p. 66.

of graduate school of longest attendance by career-bound superintendents is 1.94; the ranking is 2.42 for place-bound superintendents. The
difference between the prestige of the graduate schools attended by the
two types of superintendents yields a chi-square of 16.9 with 3 degrees
of freedom, which is significant at the .001 level of confidence.

Table 4-2

GRADUATE SCHOOLS OF SUPERINTENDENTS

TYPE OF SUPERINTENDENT	PRESTIGE OF GRADUATE SCHOOL			
	High		Low	
	1	2	3	4
Place-Bound	68	16	33	53
Career-Bound	167	36	50	50

Source: Secondary analysis of data reported by Edward S. Hickcox, "Career and Place Bound
Orientations of Chief School Officers in New York State: An Exploratory Study" (Ph.D. diss.,
Cornell University, 1966), p. 64.

An analysis of the amount of preparation and ways in which career-
and place-bound superintendents prepare for the occupation lends
credence to the implication that career-bound men have a higher commitment to the superintendency as an occupation than do place-bound
men, for it has been shown that career-bound superintendents acquire
more formal preparation and, further, they acquire such preparation
from educational institutions of higher prestige.

CAREER ORIENTATIONS

Educational Progressivism

One common factor in a career orientation is the extent to which an
individual holds *progressive* as opposed to *traditional* values regarding
the objectives of the occupation and the day-to-day work. A scale to
measure educational progressivism was developed by Neal Gross,[8] and
a secondary analysis of his raw data reveal that career-bound superintendents are more educationally progressive than place-bound superin-

---

[8] For a report of the scale see Gross, *Explorations in Role Analysis*, pp. 362-63.

tendents. Table 4–3 shows that the differences between the two types of men on the progressivism scale yields a chi-square of 9.66 with 2 degrees of freedom, significant at the .01 level of confidence.

Table 4–3

EDUCATIONAL PROGRESSIVISM OF SUPERINTENDENTS

TYPE OF SUPERINTENDENT	EDUCATIONAL PROGRESSIVISM			
	Low			High
	0	1	2	3
Place-Bound	2	10	5	16
Career-Bound	2	8	28	34

Source: Secondary analysis of data from Neal Gross, *et al., Explorations in Role Analysis* (New York: John Wiley & Sons, Inc., 1958), pp. 362–63.

Job-Career Satisfaction

The degree to which the two kinds of superintendents are satisfied with their jobs and careers differs but not significantly. Place-bound superintendents tend to be more satisfied with their jobs; however, they are less satisfied with the superintendency career. On a four-point scale measuring job satisfaction among school superintendents, a sample of 102 Massachusetts superintendents scored as follows: career-bound mean = 1.44, place-bound mean = 1.61, where the higher the score the higher the job satisfaction. The same sample measured as follows on a four-point career satisfaction scale: career-bound mean = 1.46, place-bound mean = 1.39, with the higher score the higher the satisfaction with the career of school superintendent.[9]

The patterns of these findings, though the differences are not statistically significant, are to be expected, given the higher commitment to the career on the part of career-bound men. It seems reasonable that a low commitment to a career should result in low expectations for the job and that a high commitment should result in high expectations. Thus the same job could satisfy one individual but not another, de-

---

[9] The job and career satisfaction scales are reported in Gross, *Explorations in Role Analysis*, pp. 353–54. Data reported were obtained by a secondary analysis of Gross' raw data.

pending on the person's expectation. This might explain the slight differences in job satisfaction on the part of the two types of superintendents.

Aspiration Level

Once in an occupational group, individuals generate aspiration levels that indicate the extent to which they desire to excel within the occupational framework. Statements such as "obtain a superintendency position in a larger school system" and "take a more important role in the activities of professional educational organizations" indicate these levels. A four-point scale measuring aspiration level among superintendents discriminates between career- and place-bound men and indicates that career-bound superintendents have higher aspiration levels. A sample of 102 Massachusetts superintendents revealed means of 1.7 for career-bound and 1.2 for place-bound superintendents, with the higher the score, the higher the aspiration level.[10] The difference between the two group scores on the scale is significant at the .025 level of confidence.

Aspiration level, however, is related to age; generally the older the individual, the lower the aspiration level. Those superintendents 50 and older scored a mean of 1.2, while men 49 and younger scored a mean of 1.8 on the aspiration level scale. Among superintendents 50 and over the difference on aspiration level between the two types is slight (career-bound mean = 1.3, place-bound = .95), but still shows career-bound as having higher levels of aspiration, though the difference is statistically significant only at about the .4 level of confidence.

Among superintendents 49 and younger the difference on aspiration level between the two types is large (career-bound mean = 2.05, place-bound mean = 1.6), and shows career-bound men as having higher levels of aspiration. The difference is statistically significant at the .016 level of confidence.

How One Gets Ahead

In tracing out a career an individual can develop various perspectives of his work world in relation to how one gets ahead and the justness or ethical rightness of who gets ahead. Part of this orientation involves a factor called the *active-passive* dimension. The active orientation con-

---

[10] The aspiration level scale is reported in Gross, *Explorations in Role Analysis*, p. 352. Data reported were obtained by a secondary analysis of Gross' raw data.

sists of making one's own future, of taking the initiative toward getting ahead and career movement. The passive orientation implies that one should not or need not engage the environment.

Another dimension of this orientation has been called the *idealistic-cynical* dimension. This characteristic relates to the way an individual views the ethical rightness of movement within his occupational group. The idealistically oriented person views rewards as commensurate with merit and believes that rewards are as they should be. The cynical person thinks rewards are not commensurate with merit and promotes the feeling that one must take an opportunistic view in order to get ahead. Statements such as "An individual should apply pressure toward altering a school board decision generally conflicting with his own career objectives" and "To maximize career success, one should attempt to modify the organization's objectives to fit his own" measure a school superintendent's position on the passive-active dimension of career orientation. Assertions such as "The best payoff toward career advancement comes from being expert in an area of professional competence" and "Attaining personal contacts and playing politics is what normally determines who gets ahead" bear on the idealism-cynical dimension.

The original conception and scales measuring active-passive and idealistic-cynical career orientations were developed by McKelvey [11] and utilized in research among managers, engineers, and scientists in a federal research and development unit. Following leads thus provided, Fenske developed a Guttman type scale for school administrators and administered it to a sample of Oregon school administrators.[12] What follows is a secondary analysis of that portion of data dealing with 84 school superintendents.

The two scales have a low intercorrelation, $-.08$. Moreover, they correlate to a very limited degree with factors such as age, salary, and the number of years superintendents have been in their current position. Table 4–4 shows intercorrelation among the two scales and age, salary, and years in office. The correlations are reported in the direction of the first-named element of the orientation.

Scores of career- and place-bound superintendents on the idealistic-cynical career orientation scale differ slightly, as is shown in Table 4–5.

---

[11] William W. McKelvey, "Expectational Non-Complementarity and Deviant Adaptation in a Research Organization" (Ph.D. diss., Massachusetts Institute of Technology, 1967); and Edgar H. Schein, *et al.*, "Career Orientations and Perceptions of Reward Activity in a Research Organization," *Administrative Science Quarterly*, Vol. 9 (March, 1965), 333–49.

[12] Melvin Fenske, "Career Orientation and Career Movement of School Superintendents," 1969.

Table 4-4

CORRELATIONS BETWEEN CAREER ORIENTATIONS
AND AGE, SALARY, AND YEARS IN OFFICE

| CAREER ORIENTATIONS | CAREER ORIENTATIONS | | 3 | 4 | 5 |
| | 1 | 2 | AGE | SALARY | YEARS |
	IDEALISM-CYNICAL	ACTIVE-PASSIVE			IN PRESENT POSITION
1 *Idealism*-cynical	1.000	−.08	+.009	−.062	+.112
2 *Active*-passive	−.08	1.00	+.131	−.030	+.098

Source: Secondary analysis of data reported by Melvin Fenske, "Career Orientation and Career Movement of School Superintendents," 1969.

Table 4-5

IDEALISTIC-CYNICAL CAREER ORIENTATION
OF SUPERINTENDENTS *

| CAREER ORIENTATION | TYPE OF SUPERINTENDENT [Number and (Percentage)] | | |
	Place-Bound	Career-Bound	Total
Idealistic	19 (48.7)	23 (51.1)	42 (50)
Ambivalent	18 (46.2)	20 (44.4)	38 (45.2)
Cynical	2 (5.1)	2 (4.4)	4 (4.8)

* Idealistic = 5 or 4, Ambivalent = 3 or 2, Cynical = 1 or 0.

Source: Secondary analysis of data reported by Melvin Fenske, "Career Orientation and Career Movement of School Superintendents," 1969.

The means are 3.41 for place-bound superintendents and 3.55 for the career-bound. Notable about the distribution is the heavy loading toward the idealistic end of the continuum.

Scores of the two types of superintendents on the active-passive career orientation scale do differ. As shown in Table 4-6, career-bound

Table 4–6

ACTIVE-PASSIVE CAREER ORIENTATION OF SUPERINTENDENTS *

CAREER ORIENTATIONS	TYPE OF SUPERINTENDENT [Number and (Percentage)]		
	Place-Bound	Career-Bound	Total
Active	6	14	20
	(15.4)	(31)	(23.7)
Ambivalent	21	21	42
	(53.4)	(46.7)	(50)
Passive	12	10	22
	(30.8)	(22.2)	(26.2)

* Active = 5 or 4, Ambivalent = 3 or 2, Passive = 1 or 0.

Source: Secondary analysis of data reported by Melvin Fenske, "Career Orientation and Career Movement of School Superintendents," 1969.

men have a more active orientation than do place-bound ones. A Mann-Whitney U test produces a one-tail p of .035 which indicates a statistically significant difference in the scores of the two types at the .035 level of confidence. Aside from indicating that career-bound men have a more active career orientation, the data indicate a slight loading toward the passive career style for the total group. Both tables show a tendency for all superintendents in the sample to have an idealistic-passive career orientation.

Combining the two scales, as shown in Table 4–7, affords another view of the two types of superintendents. Taking into account only those superintendents at the extreme ends of the career orientation continua, and ignoring the *ambivalent* category, Table 4–7 shows that when extreme scores or "pure types" are considered, the most prevalent career orientation of the place-bound superintendents is the ritualistic orientation (idealistic and passive) and the crusading orientation (idealistic and active) is the most prevalent orientation among the career-bound superintendents.

Mobility

The differences in career styles noted to this point bear on the way in which the decision to enter the occupation was made, preparation for the career educational progressivism, level of career aspiration, job and career satisfaction, and the career orientations of idealism-cynical and active-passive. The analysis now deals with occupational mobility as viewed by the two types. It would be expected that career-bound superintendents would see mobility as a positive or natural element of the career in as much as mobility has played a greater part in their career trace than it has among place-bound superintendents.

Table 4–7

CAREER ORIENTATION OF SUPERINTENDENTS *

| | TYPE OF SUPERINTENDENT | |
CAREER ORIENTATION	Place-Bound	Career-Bound
Crusading (active-idealistic)	1	8
Ritualistic (passive-idealistic)	6	3
Insurgent (active-cynical)	0	2
Retreatist (passive-cynical)	1	0

* Active = 5 or 4, Ambivalent = 3 or 2, Passive = 1 or 0. Idealistic = 5 or 4, Ambivalent = 3 or 2, Cynical = 1 or 0.

Source: Secondary analysis of data reported by Melvin Fenske, "Career Orientation and Career Movement of School Superintendents," 1969.

Table 4–8 shows the mean responses of a sample of Oregon school superintendents to some questions bearing on mobility within the superintendency. Responses to the questions were elicited and scored in the form of a continuum from strongly disagree (1) to strongly agree (6). The table also shows the predicted direction of the difference between the means for career- and place-bound superintendents. Over-

Table 4–8

MOBILITY AND TYPE OF SUPERINTENDENT

MOBILITY STATEMENTS	MEAN SCORE		PREDICTION	SIGN
	C.B.	P.B.		
1. The increased pressure would make me hesitant to move to a superintendency with more responsibility.	2.4	2.6	C.B.<P.B.	+
2. I would advise a young man entering the superintendency to find a satisfactory position as soon as possible and remain there until retirement.	1.6	1.8	C.B.<P.B.	+

Table 4–8 (Cont.)

MOBILITY STATEMENTS	MEAN SCORE		PREDICTION	SIGN
	C.B.	P.B.		
3. A superintendent who plans to get ahead in the profession must be willing to move his family.	5.2	4.9	C.B.>P.B.	+
4. If I had started a major project in my district I would feel an obligation to remain in the district until its completion even if I were offered a much better job.	3.5	4.0	C.B.<P.B.	+
5. A person owes it to himself and his family to watch constantly for better job opportunities.	3.3	3.8	C.B.>P.B.	−
6. My career plans have always been to advance to more important district superintendencies.	2.6	2.8	C.B.>P.B.	−
7. The job should come before family for a superintendent in his decision to move elsewhere.	2.9	2.4	C.B.>P.B.	+
8. Career success for the school superintendent does not necessarily involve his moving from district to district.	4.7	5.0	C.B.<P.B.	+
9. A superintendent who has his mind on a better position for himself cannot do justice to his present job.	2.4	2.5	C.B.<P.B.	+
10. I would not move to a better job if I felt such a move would be detrimental to the district in which I am now employed.	3.4	3.4	C.B.<P.B.	0
11. I would not let my friendship ties in a community stand in the way of moving on to a better superintendency.	3.6	3.4	C.B.>P.B.	+
12. It is difficult to name truly successful superintendents who have not held two or more superintendencies during their career.	4.4	3.1	C.B.>P.B.	+

Source: Secondary analysis of data reported in Robert L. Rose, "Career-Bound; Place-Bound: An Attitude Study of the Superintendency," 1967.

all, the data indicate that career-bound men are more favorably inclined toward mobility. A sign test reveals the difference to be significant at the .033 level of confidence on a one-tail test.

Another measure of attitude toward mobility involves the superintendent's desire or lack of desire to stay in their present superintendencies until retirement. Table 4–9 shows the distribution of the attitudes by age and by type of superintendent held by a sample of Oregon school superintendents.

Table 4–9

AGE GROUPS, TYPE OF SUPERINTENDENT AND DESIRE TO REMAIN IN PRESENT SUPERINTENDENCY UNTIL RETIREMENT

AGE GROUPS	SUPERINTENDENTS EXPRESSING DESIRE TO REMAIN IN PRESENT SUPERINTENDENCY UNTIL RETIREMENT [Percentage and (Number)]			
	Career-Bound		Place-Bound	
40 and under	0%	(12)	25%	(4)
41-45	17	(6)	20	(5)
46-50	25	(8)	62.5	(8)
51-55	50	(8)	50	(6)
56-60	87.5	(16)	100	(7)
61 and over	100	(3)	–	(0)

Source: Secondary analysis of data reported in Robert L. Rose, "Career-Bound; Place-Bound: An Attitude Study of the Superintendency," 1967.

As would be expected, desire to remain in the present superintendency until retirement is related to age. And ignoring age, there is only a slight difference between the two groups. In total, 45 per cent of the career-bound and 57 per cent of the place-bound superintendents wish to stay in their current superintendencies until retirement. However, the desire to remain until retirement is expressed more often by place-bound than by career-bound men among those 50 years of age and younger. The difference in the expression of the desire is statistically significant at .031 level of confidence on a one-tail test. The desire to remain in the present superintendency is expressed with rather equal frequency by both types among those men over 50 years old.

Both measures of mobility discussed are questions of attitudes. A further view of the general dimension of mobility among the two types concerns action—not mobility itself, but the serious contemplation to move to a new superintendency. Involving oneself in an interview with a school board about a superintendency vacancy seemingly would be undertaken only after considerable deliberation. This action clearly calls for contemplation about the prospect of career movement and probably would be undertaken only when one's ascertained attitudes to the prospect were at least neutral, rather than negative. In a sample of 83 Oregon superintendents, 26 (about 31 per cent) of the men indicated that within the preceding two years they had been interviewed by a school board regarding possible appointment to a different superintendency. Thirty-four per cent of the career-bound and 13 per cent of the place-bound superintendents said that they had been interviewed for a superintendency. The difference is statistically significant beyond the .05 level of confidence on a one-tail test. One might expect the frequency of such interviews to be related to age; however, the sample failed to show a significant relationship. Even though frequency declined slightly with age, it was rather uniformly distributed among age groups.

Career Anchorage Point

An individual ruminating about his career might be moved to sum it up by suggesting that he had come a long way or he might say that he still had a long way to go. In the first instance one might say that the man was *downward anchored,* and in the second, that he was *upward anchored* in terms of his career success. Rose developed a six-point Guttman-type scale to measure career anchorage points among school superintendents and administered it to a sample of 72 Oregon superintendents.[13] Table 4–10 shows the distribution of career- and place-

Table 4–10

CAREER ANCHORAGE POINTS OF SUPERINTENDENTS*

CAREER ANCHORAGE POINT	TYPE OF SUPERINTENDENT	
	Career-Bound	Place-Bound
Upward	2	2
Ambivalent	10	4
Downward	38	16

* Upward = 6 or 5; Ambivalent = 4, 3, or 2; Downward = 1 or 0.

Source: Secondary analysis of data reported in Robert L. Rose, "Career-Bound; Place-Bound: An Attitude Study of the Superintendency," 1967.

[13] Data are based on a secondary analysis of results from Robert L. Rose, "Career-Bound; Place-Bound: An Attitude Study of the Superintendency," 1967.

bound superintendents according to career anchorage point. The slight difference between the two types shows the mean career anchorage point is 1.24 for career-bound and 1.14 for place-bound superintendents. Most notable about the distribution is the marked downward anchorage orientation.

Two assumptions about career anchorage points seem reasonable: the older should be more downward anchored, and those having achieved desired superintendencies should be more downward anchored than those in superintendencies that are not so desirable.[14] But, as shown in Table 4–11, neither assumption holds up. Because the career anchorage point scale fails to show a consistent relationship to

Table 4–11

AGE, SALARY, AND CAREER ANCHORAGE POINT OF SUPERINTENDENTS*

AGE GROUPS	MEAN CAREER ANCHORAGE POINT	SALARY LEVEL	MEAN CAREER ANCHORAGE POINT
45 and under	1.62	7	.5
		6	1.0
46–55	0.78	5	2.3
		4	.8
56 and over	1.45	3	1.6
		2	1.3
		1	0

* Upward = 6 or 5; Ambivalent = 4, 3, or 2; Downward = 1 or 0.

Source: Secondary analysis of data reported in Robert L. Rose, "Career-Bound; Place-Bound: An Attitude Study of the Superintendency," 1967.

age, and since Tausky and Dubin, the creators of the measure of which Rose's scale is a modification, report a strong relationship between age and career anchorage point,[15] one might suspect the validity of the Rose scale. Further, even though the Rose scale is a scale and possesses all the characteristics of a good Guttman scale, it fails to discriminate among superintendents; only about 6 per cent of the sample falls within the upward anchorage range while 75 per cent of the sample falls within the downward anchorage range. On the other hand, the Rose

---

[14] Desirability of a superintendency or, more precisely, prestige of a superintendency, has an extremely high correlation with salary paid. See Mason and Gross, "Intra-Occupational Prestige Differentiation."

[15] See Curt Tausky and Robert Dubin, "Career Anchorage: Managerial Mobility Motivations," *American Sociological Review*, Vol. 30 (October, 1965), 725–35.

scale might be highly valid; age might not be related to career anchorage point among school superintendents, and the scale might possess high capacity to discriminate. These matters cannot be settled with the available data.

Reference Group Orientation

Reference groups set norms for an individual; they can determine the individual's standards. And reference groups can be placed in a hierarchy in terms of their importance to a given individual. Because reference groups may influence the work of an individual, the reference-group orientation of school superintendents is important in the attempt to describe the career styles of career- and place-bound superintendents.

A sample of 144 superintendents from Oregon and Pennsylvania was asked, "Whose estimate of your work is most important to you?" and then asked to rank order the following groups: local community groups, my administrative staff, my teachers, my school board, other school superintendents, and others to be specified. In asking this question it was assumed that because the place-bound superintendent has risen from the ranks of teachers and administrators in the containing organization and since the teachers and administrators were to some extent involved in his rise to the superintendency, place-bound superintendents would rank teachers and administrative staff higher than they would be ranked by career-bound superintendents. Place-bound men gave a mean rank of 1.9 to teachers and 2.5 to administrative staff, and career-bound men gave them mean ranks respectively of 2.4 and 2.8. Viewed differently, 59 per cent of the place-bound and 43 per cent of the career-bound men ranked either their teachers or their administrative staff at the top of the hierarchy of reference groups. The difference is statistically significant at the .05 level of confidence on a one-tail test.

As an indicator of the potential influence of reference groups in shaping one's views and actions it is possible to see a relationship between the high ranking place-bound men give teachers and their attitudes toward teachers. When a sample of 473 New York State superintendents was asked to name the chief obstacle to improving educational opportunity in their school systems, career-bound superintendents named teachers more frequently than did place-bound superintendents. Among the superintendents, the percentage naming teachers as the chief obstacle were 14 per cent of the place-bound and 20 per cent of the career-bound superintendents. The difference is significant at the .05 level on a one-tail test.

Career Style

Having examined differences between career- and place-bound superintendents it is possible, by way of summary, to speak of their different career styles. Once in public education, the typical career-bound superintendent aims from the beginning for the top of the hierarchy—the superintendency. He sets his sights high and early and views positions below his goal as steps toward the superintendency. Preparing for the career, he is active and acquires his graduate training early, to the fullest extent, and from the better institutions of higher education.

The place-bound superintendent, on the other hand, gradually escalates his occupational aspirations. His desire for the superintendency develops late and frequently appears only when the opportunity does. He sees positions below the superintendency as ends in themselves. As he fills positions of increasing responsibility and finds success, he gradually escalates his aspirations and one day finds himself in the superintendency. In pursuit of preparation he is less active than his counterpart, tends to drag out his preparation period, and secure his preparation on a part-time basis. Further he tends to acquire less than the maximum preparation and is not very particular about the prestige of the place offering the formal graduate school preparation.

The career-bound superintendent holds a more progressive view about education and aspires to greater prominence among superintendents than does his counterpart. In viewing his job he tends to be less satisfied. Regarding his career, the career-bound superintendent finds it slightly more satisfying; he sees mobility, to a greater extent, as a desired or natural element of the career; he feels more strongly that one must take an active part in the pursuit of career objectives—one must confront the environment if one is to get ahead; and he tends to hold less limited success criteria of career judgment than his counterpart.

5

Successors: Position in the Social Structure of Superintendents

Place- and career-bound superintendents exhibit different career styles; moreover, they occupy differing positions in the social structure among their peers—among school superintendents. It is the purpose of this chapter to detail the difference in the positions held in the social structure by the two types. This will be done through an analysis of status, social network involvement, and the flow of communications.

Data for this chapter come almost exclusively from a sample of 61 out of 63 superintendents in Allegheny County, Pennsylvania. Although terms in office varied, all of the men in the sample had been in office at least two years when the data were secured. And besides having at least two years to establish relationships, the men met together monthly and their work activities afforded numerous contacts with each other.

SOCIAL NETWORK INVOLVEMENT

Social structure is defined in terms of the distribution and differentiation of status, roles, and patterns of interaction or communication among members of a group. Differentiation of status, in part, sets up patterns of interaction. Members of a group do not fit into the social network of interaction at random; some are heavily and consistently involved in it, while others are only loosely and spasmodically connected. In looking at the social network of inter-action among superintendents we want to see the extent of involvement of career- and place-bound men.

When the men in the sample were asked to name their three best friends among the other members of the sample, the choices were un-equally divided between the two types of superintendents. The mean number of times named as a friendship choice was 3.43 for career-bound and 2.18 for place-bound superintendents. Table 5–1 shows the

Table 5–1

FRIENDSHIP CHOICES OF SUPERINTENDENTS

TYPE OF SUPERINTENDENT	NUMBER OF FRIENDSHIP CHOICES RECEIVED		
	0–1	2–3	4 or more
Career-Bound	9	5	14
Place-Bound	15	13	5

distribution of friendship choices received by the two types. The differ-ence yields a chi-square value of 9.05 with 2 degrees of freedom, signifi-cant at the .02 level of confidence.[1]

No evidence indicates that the two types constitute closed groups or that one group chooses rather exclusively from its own type. On the contrary, each group of superintendents named many of the other group as friendship choices, but not equally. The sample consisting of 33 place- and 28 career-bound superintendents showed that the latter rather evenly split their choices. The place-bound men, however, gave almost twice as many friendship choices to career-bound men. Ob-viously, then, place-bound men respond more favorably to career-bound men as friends than they do to their own type; over-all, career-bound superintendents received significantly more friendship choices.

The number of friendship choices a man receives helps indicate his involvement in the social network of interaction among superintendents. Clearly, men who receive many choices are more involved in the social network. Also indicative of involvement in the social network is the

---

[1] When time in office is controlled even further, the means among those in office at least six years were as follows: Career-bound = 4.18, Place-bound = 2.90.

amount of interaction one has with the group. Sample members were asked to estimate the relative amount of their interaction with the other superintendents. It was reasoned that high interaction in the network would permit superintendents to give accurate judgments about events in other school systems. It was further assumed that men who were involved would be able to make an accurate judgment as to whether their system had adopted more or fewer innovations than the county average. (Concurrent investigation yielded the mean adoption rate for the school systems in the county.)

An additional measure of involvement in the social network of interaction stems from a professionalism ranking (which will be described fully in the next section). The sample members were asked to rank the professionalism of every member in the sample. With some frequency, the subjects reported "no opinion" about a given man. The number of times an individual received a "no opinion" response presumably indicated his level of social network involvement. Thus, four measures of involvement in the social network of interaction were generated: number of friendship choices received, perception of amount of interaction, accuracy of judgment, and the number of times ranked "no opinion" on a professionalism ranking.

These four measures composed a ranking scheme for involvement in the social network of interaction. Except for the *accuracy of judgment* measure, the distributions were split at the mean and all above the mean were ranked high and all below were ranked low. Those whose judgment was accurate were ranked high, and those whose judgment was inaccurate were ranked low. Table 5–2 shows the distribution of high ranking on the four measures by the two types of superintendents. The mean ranking was 2.4 for the career-bound superintendents and

Table 5–2

SUPERINTENDENT'S INVOLVEMENT IN THE SOCIAL NETWORK OF INTERACTION

TYPE OF SUPERINTENDENT	NUMBER OF HIGH RANKINGS ON FOUR INVOLVEMENT MEASURES				
	1 (4 highs)	2 (3 highs)	3 (2 highs)	4 (1 high)	5 (0 highs)
Career-Bound	11	6	4	3	4
Place-Bound	4	5	3	10	11

3.6 for place-bound superintendents. The difference in the distribution of the ranks of the two types yields a Mann-Whitney U with a z value of 2.72 which is significant at the .007 level of confidence. Therefore, career-bound superintendents are significantly more involved in the social network of interaction of superintendents than are place-bound men.

STATUS

Not only do the two types differ regarding their involvement in the social network of interaction, they differ in their status in the social structure.

Four indicators of status were used to construct a ranking system: amount of education, prestige of the superintendency held, opinion leadership, and professionalism.

Amount of education was assessed directly. Men with a Ph.D. or Ed.D. were ranked high and those with less formal education were ranked low. And, as we have seen, career-bound men attain more education than do place-bound men. Prestige of the superintendency held was determined by the salary paid. (As indicated earlier, salary is a reliable predictor of prestige.) An opinion-leadership score was obtained by asking members of the sample to give the names of all individuals they had deliberately contacted for advice or information about educational practices within a 10-month period. Thus a score was compiled of the number of times each sample member had been sought out for advice or information. To obtain a professionalism score, every sample member was offered a deck of cards; each card contained the name of one member of the sample. The superintendents were then to sort the cards into six piles according to the professionalism exhibited by the individual. One pile contained names of individuals on which the rater could reach no opinion. The sorting was done after each superintendent was asked to "indicate the characteristics of the truly professional school superintendent" and some general non-directive discussion of ideas had taken place. The distributions of scores on prestige, opinion leadership, and professionalism were split at the means; those above the mean were ranked high and those below it, low.

Table 5–3 shows the distribution of high rankings on these measures of status for the two types of superintendents. The mean rank for career-bound men is 2.6, and the mean rank for place-bound men is 3.7. The difference in the distribution yields a Mann-Whitney U with a z value of 2.46, which is significant at the .014 level of confidence.

Thus career- and place-bound men hold differing positions in the so-

Table 5–3

STATUS RANKINGS OF SUPERINTENDENTS

TYPE OF SUPERINTENDENT	NUMBER OF HIGH RANKINGS ON FOUR STATUS MEASURES				
	1 (4 highs)	2 (3 highs)	3 (2 highs)	4 (1 high)	5 (0 highs)
Career-Bound	12	4	2	3	7
Place-Bound	2	3	9	8	11

cial structure of school superintendents. Career-bound men are significantly more involved in the network of interaction of the social structure and hold significantly higher status in the social structure of school superintendents.

THE FLOW OF COMMUNICATION

Information flowing through communication channels is vital to any occupational group. The kind or quality of information available to various occupational groups, however, varies. Farmers and physicians, for example, often rely on information based on scientific experiments and observations to help them decide among alternatives in problem solving. Other occupational groups—school superintendents included—deal mainly with information which lacks an empirical base; they must depend on folklore or conventional wisdom.

For example, assume that a school system considers adopting a new educational practice. By reading professional journals, surveying the mass media, and conversing with experts and others, educators can generally obtain assertions by one and all about the value of the new practice, revelations of nonsystematic observations, and recalled tales of experience. As soft and flabby as it is, this kind of information is about all the school superintendent has to rely on. Given this type of information, the assumed credibility and authority of the purveyor are cardinal points. Thus in their active search for information, superintendents seek out credible informants through reading, through attending meetings, conferences, and seminars, and through personal contact. The extensiveness of the search for information is of prime concern here; more particularly, the degree to which the two types of superintendents seek information and, in turn, dispense it, is of importance.

Superintendents often seek information at the numerous meetings and conferences they attend. These gatherings not only have organized programs for dispensing of information, they also afford opportunities for person-to-person exchanges. The sample members, after consulting their calendars and memories, listed the number of professional meetings and conferences they had attended outside Allegheny County over a 10-month period. An interest in the flow of information to the county prompted the selection of meetings outside. Table 5–4 shows the number of such meetings attended by career- and place-bound superintendents. Career-bound men, on the average, attended 50 per cent more meetings than did place-bound men. The difference in the distribution

Table 5–4

SUPERINTENDENTS' ATTENDANCE AT PROFESSIONAL MEETINGS

NUMBER OF MEETINGS	TYPE OF SUPERINTENDENT	
	Career-Bound	Place-Bound
0–2	2	9
3–5	17	18
6–8	6	4
9 or more	3	2

yields a Mann-Whitney U with a z value of 1.97, which is significant at the .05 level of confidence. As measured by attendance at professional meetings and to the extent to which such meetings are a prime source of information, it can be seen that career-bound men are most active in securing and bringing information into the county.

Another way of seeking information and making it available within the county is to deliberately seek out some individual outside the county for advice and information. The sample members reported on this activity, and the frequency distributions are shown in Table 5–5. Over-all, career-bound superintendents communicated with such informants three times more than did place-bound men. The difference in the distributions yields a Mann-Whitney U with a z value of 2.53, significant at the .01 level of confidence.

After measuring two ways information about educational practices travels to the county, it is obvious that career-bound superintendents act as information vehicles. And because they are instrumental in securing the information, are of higher status, and are more involved in the social network, they should be the principal dispensers of infor-

Table 5–5

SEEKING OF ADVICE FROM PERSONS OUTSIDE THE COUNTY BY SUPERINTENDENTS

NUMBER OF TIMES INFORMANTS WERE CONTACTED	TYPE OF SUPERINTENDENT	
	Career-Bound	Place-Bound
0	11	21
1	5	8
2	4	3
3	4	1
4 or more	4	0

mation and advice. Again, interview data shows that career-bound superintendents were asked for advice and information almost three times as often as were place-bound men (59 and 22 contacts respectively). Table 5–6 shows the frequency distributions on advice and information given by type of superintendent. The difference in the distributions yields a Mann-Whitney U with a z value of 2.34, which is significant at the .01 level on a one-tail test.

Table 5–6

REQUESTS FOR INFORMATION FROM SUPERINTENDENTS

NUMBER OF TIMES ASKED FOR INFORMATION	TYPE OF SUPERINTENDENT	
	Career-Bound	Place-Bound
0–1	15	28
2–3	6	7
4–5	4	1
6 or more	3	1

Obviously then, career- and place-bound superintendents occupy different positions in the social structure of school superintendents. The data indicate that career-bound superintendents occupy a higher place in the social order, enjoy higher status, and involve themselves more in the social network of interaction. Moreover, the flow of information about educational practices is largely accomplished by career-bound superintendents.

AASA Elected Officers

Besides achieving high local status, superintendents have opportunities to achieve high status in the nationwide professional organization of school superintendents, the American Association of School Administrators. Members of the AASA elect individuals to three offices, President, Vice-president and Executive committee. The elections are taken quite seriously. Campaign managers are appointed and votes are solicited widely through printed circulars and other means.

The data about the varying positions in the social structure of school superintendents in Allegheny County suggest that career-bound superintendents would be elected to AASA offices more frequently than would place-bound superintendents. And this is indeed the case. From 1960 to 1969, 29 individuals were elected to one of the three AASA offices. Twenty-eight of them were school superintendents and 24 were career-bound superintendents. Since a large national sample of superintendents shows that 31 per cent are place-bound and 68 per cent are career-bound, chance expectations indicate that 8.76 place-bound men and 19.24 career-bound men would be elected to office. The differences between the observed and expected frequencies yield a chi-square value of 3.77, which is significant at the .026 level of confidence on a one-tail test.

It can be seen, then, that not only does the career-bound superintendent occupy a higher place in the social order of superintendents at the local level, he also more frequently occupies a higher status at the national level, as measured by office holding in the national professional association of school superintendents.

6

Selection of Successor and Conditions of Employment

School superintendents are not all alike. Their origins in terms of the containing organization differ, which affects their varying commitments to place of employment as opposed to the occupation of school superintendent. These varying commitments, in turn, are reflected in career decisions, career preparation, and career orientations or styles. And they are also reflected in achieved position in the social structure of school superintendents.

When school board members replace a superintendent, they must make a choice between types of superintendents. It is the making of this choice on which this chapter centers. When this stage in the succession cycle occurs, assessment of the state of affairs of the organization takes on new intensity. Judgments are made about the organization's condition, about its recent performance, and about its leadership needs for future achievement. The outcome of this reflection has a direct bearing on whether a career- or place-bound man is hired and on the conditions of his employment.

Decision Contingencies

A school board has considerable freedom when hiring a superintendent. Seniority rights have no direct bearing on the appointment. No review occurs at a higher level. To be sure, an applicant may have people lobby to the board, but no official pressure can be applied. The board can make the appointment solely in terms of what it believes will be best for itself and the school system. The questions, then, are under what conditions school boards deem it best to appoint a place-bound man as the new superintendent and when they deem it best to have a career-bound superintendent?

Observations and interviews in four school systems where case studies were conducted helped to formulate the following propositions about appointment: If the administration of the school system is perceived as unsatisfactory, the appointment will go to a career-bound man. If the administration is perceived as satisfactory by the school board, the appointment will go to either type.[1] It is natural for school boards to call on a place-bound superintendent when things are going well. After all, he knows the school system and its history and undoubtedly is well informed of its programs, problems, sources of support, philosophy, and personnel.

Sometimes, however, no one from within the school system has the necessary experience or credentials to be given the superintendency. When this situation occurs, the call must go to someone from outside. Someone from outside is also often brought in when the opposite is true, when there are too many from within who are qualified. Selecting one from among them might invite unnecessary grievances and perhaps high-level sabotage, or might deepen the rift between already existing factions so as to create serious consequences. It seems that when all is going well the choice of either type of superintendent has some such reasonable explanation.

These assumptions hold up when matched with the experience in the

---

[1] The central idea of these propositions is that at the time of dissatisfaction or crisis a group or an organization will seek something from which it is not currently benefiting to solve its problem and that a satisfied group or organization will seek to perpetuate the situation in which it is satisfied. Such propositions derive support from the small-group experimental situation. Hamblin reports a study involving three-person college student groups in competition with "high school students" in a game of modified shuffle board. Scores of both teams were posted as they played. A "crisis" was produced by secretly altering the rules of scoring for the college groups only which enabled the high school groups to score more frequently. It was found that the groups experiencing the crisis were significantly more likely to replace their leaders. See R. L. Hamblin, "Leadership and Crisis," *Sociometry*, Vol. 21 (December, 1958), 322–35.

districts under observation and with histories collected on 36 other successions. In a sample of 36 succession cases, no place-bound superintendent reported that the school board was unhappy with the way the schools were being administered at the time of his appointment. Typical responses were: "I succeeded a very successful man" or "I think they were satisfied. Now you'll always have an individual who is dissatisfied with a particular part of a school system but generally they seemed to be proud." In no case where the situation was defined as unsatisfactory had a place-bound man been appointed.

Not only do reports of school superintendents confirm the notion that only career-bound men are hired when a judgment has been rendered that organizational performance is less than it could be, data about the internal state of affairs of school boards also confirm the finding. Most school board members are elected by district voters. As reflected by voter turnout, citizens are seldom excited about school board elections. Few citizens see it as a highly prized post. Contestants for the office are few, largely self-recruited, and most often unnoted for their activity in local political parties.

School board members' reasons for seeking office often come under scrutiny. Table 6–1 displays their motives. Reasons listed 1 through 7 can be interpreted as representing varying degrees of dissatisfaction with the schools; these reasons, taken together, are offered with considerable frequency. This should be expected. In most elections office seekers indicate that the position is not being properly handled and imply that they will do better. And while challengers are doing this, incumbents are "standing on their records" as justification for their re-election.

When a challenger defeats an incumbent, the majority of the voters obviously believed, as did the winner, that a gap existed between performance and expectations regarding the school system. And, further, the challenger feels he has a mandate to strive for improvement. Thus, when a school board contains such a new member, the presence of his presumed mandate might have a bearing on the selection of a successor to the superintendency when that situation arises. Thus a board containing a victorious challenger includes at least one member somewhat committed to the notion that all is not right with the school system; and if his stance gains favor with the other members, then the successor would be career-bound.

Freeborn, following this reasoning, put the problem to a test.[2] He

---

[2] See Robert M. Freeborn, "School Board Change and the Succession Pattern of Superintendents" (Ph.D. diss., Claremont Graduate School, 1966).

Table 6–1

REASONS FOR SEEKING ELECTION AMONG BOARD MEMBERS

REASON FOR SEEKING ELECTION	PERCENTAGE OF BOARD MEMBERS ($N = 508$)
1. Felt that someone had to see that school expenditures were increased	12
2. Wanted certain friends to get in or advance in the school system	1
3. Felt that the school superintendent should be removed	5
4. A certain group in the community felt that they should be represented on the school board	26
5. Felt that someone had to see that school expenditures were decreased	4
6. Did not like the way his children were being educated	11
7. Disapproved of the way the schools were being run	20
8. Felt it to be his civic duty	80
9. Was interested in getting some experience in politics	9
10. Other	48

Source: Neal Gross, *Who Runs Our Schools?* (New York: John Wiley & Sons, Inc., 1958), p. 73.

located 121 cases of succession in the superintendency over 9 years in 117 school systems. In each of the 121 cases he determined whether or not, within the three years preceding the replacement of the school superintendent, a school board member had been defeated at the polls or recalled. When such an event had occurred, he labeled the board a "change" board. If the event had not occurred, he labeled the board a "no change" board. Then he noted the origin of the successors chosen by the two types of boards.

Table 6–2 shows the results of his work. Change boards display an overwhelming preference for career-bound men. The difference in the type of school superintendents selected by the two board types yields a chi-square of 20.41, which is significant beyond the .001 level of confidence.

Table 6–2

SCHOOL BOARD TYPES AND SUPERINTENDENTS

SCHOOL BOARD TYPE	SUPERINTENDENT TYPE	
	Place-Bound	Career-Bound
No change	33	28
Change	9	51

Source: Robert M. Freeborn, "School Board Change and the Succession Pattern of Superintendents" (Ph.D. diss., Claremont Graduate School, 1966).

A similar line of research was carried out by Schafer[3] among recently consolidated school systems where several school boards were disbanded and a new, single school board elected. The members elected for the consolidated school system were often boardsmen from the parent school systems. Schafer measured the extent to which the new school board contained boardsmen who had served with school systems before they were consolidated. Again, it was assumed that the less the consolidated board reflected the component boards, the greater was the dissatisfaction with the schools.

A top priority of the board in a newly consolidated system is to select a school superintendent. As with board members in the component systems, the several superintendents no longer held superintendencies. One among them must be selected, or someone must be brought in from outside the consolidated system. Schafer's research among 54 newly consolidated systems shows that the less the new school board membership reflects the component boards' make-up, the more often a man from outside the consolidated system was selected as superintendent; the more the new board reflects the component boards,

---

[3] See Eldon Schafer, "Unification: A Change of Power Structure Reflected in Board Composition and Superintendent Selection" (Ph.D. diss., Claremont Graduate School, 1966).

the more often a man from within the consolidated system was selected as superintendent.[4]

Thus when school board members are dissatisfied with the performance of the school system, they hire a career-bound superintendent; they go outside the district for new leadership. The conditions of employment, in part, indicate that school board members will be satisfied if the place-bound man maintains the status quo, but they expect and are only satisfied with a career-bound man when changes are made. School boards, then, hope for a *creative* performance from a career-bound man, but are happy with a *stabilizing* performance from a place-bound man.

MANDATE

In a real sense the career-bound superintendent receives a mandate from the school board. Often hired when the board is dissatisfied with the administration of the schools, he is given a mandate to act. The place-bound man, hired only when satisfaction with the schools exists, is less likely to be given a mandate. This distinction in the working relationship with school boards is demonstrated by superintendents' responses to the question: "What kind of a superintendent was the school committee looking for when they hired you?"

The responses of 105 Massachusetts school superintendents to this open-ended question were analyzed, phrase by phrase, and placed in descriptive categories.[5] Of the 152 responses, all but 13 fit into one of three categories: (1) improvement desired, (2) action desired, and (3) personal characteristics. The latter category is self-explanatory; the distinction between the first and the second, although they both call for action and give direction, hinges on improvement, and only if improvement or a simile was used in connection with the action specified was the response recorded in first category. For example, if a superintendent responded by saying the board wanted someone to improve public relations, the response was scored "improvement desired"; if he responded by saying that the board wanted good public relations, it was scored "action desired."

---

[4] Note that Schafer's work does not connect directly with career- and place-bound superintendents as defined here. His work is a more general test among school systems of the notion that a "crisis" calls for new leadership brought in from outside the organization.

[5] The material presented here is based on a secondary analysis of raw data collected by Gross for his *Explorations in Role Analysis*.

The categories were imposed on the responses, and superintendents could and did respond so that responses could be scored in all categories or several times in one category. Table 6–3 shows the distribution of responses by type of superintendent.

Table 6–3

SUPERINTENDENTS AND REASONS APPOINTED TO OFFICE

REASON APPOINTED TO OFFICE	TYPE OF SUPERINTENDENT	
	Career-Bound	Place-Bound
1. *Improvement Desired*		
discipline	1	2
staff relations	5	0
public relations	7	0
instructional program	14	2
general, unspecified	9	3
2. *Action Desired*		
perpetuate current program	2	5
keep costs low	1	1
good business practices	2	3
start building program	8	0
conciliatory	4	1
3. *Personal Characteristics*		
knowledge of local problems	0	7
good past performance	2	8
personality	13	6
education	4	1
experience	18	2
religion	0	1
age	5	2

Source: Secondary analysis of data reported by Neal Gross, *et al.*, *Explorations of Role Analysis* (New York: John Wiley & Sons, Inc., 1958).

Responses from 38 per cent of the career- and 16 per cent of the place-bound superintendents fell into the "improvement desired" category. About 61 per cent of the responses of place-bound and about 44 per cent of the responses of career-bound men fell in the "personal characteristics" category.

As indicated, thirteen elements of the responses could not be placed into any of the categories. They were as follows: *career-bound:* wanted a man with common sense—wanted information about the schools; *place-bound:* doubt that they had any specific qualifications in mind, appointment was not conducted on a professional basis, wanted a community-minded man, school board didn't ask me any questions, they just wanted someone to be the superintendent, didn't set up any standards, there was no interview with the committee, just offered me the position, wanted a man at the cheapest price, wanted a middle-of-the-road man.

Table 6–4 analyzes the data to test the notion that the career-bound more frequently than the place-bound superintendent receives a mandate from the school board. Category 5 in the table is the number of men not responding to the question; category 4 reports the number giving "residual" response, those responses reported above. Those counted in category 3 responded only with personal characteristics; those in category 2 specified some action desired, and sometimes some personal characteristics as well; those in category 1 specified some improvement desired and sometimes some action and some personal characteristics.

Table 6–4

SUPERINTENDENTS AND REASONS APPOINTED TO OFFICE

TYPE OF RESPONSE	TYPE OF SUPERINTENDENT	
	Career-Bound	Place-Bound
1. Improvement Desired	34	5
2. Action Desired	10	5
3. Personal Characteristics	14	11
4. Residual	2	11
5. No Response	11	2

Source: Secondary analysis of data reported by Neal Gross, *et al., Explorations of Role Analysis* (New York: John Wiley & Sons, Inc., 1958).

The most liberal definition of *mandate* would be to include both "improvement desired" and "action desired" categories. Assuming this definition, among those responding, 44 career-bound men reported a mandate response and 16 did not; 10 place-bound men reported a "mandate" response and 22 did not. Using this distribution, a chi-square test yields a value of 13.6, significant at the .001 level of confidence.

A more restrictive definition of *mandate* includes only those in the "improvement desired" category. Among those responding, 34 career-bound superintendents reported a mandate and 26 did not, and 5 place-bound superintendents reported a mandate and 27 did not. Using this distribution, a chi-square test yields a value of 12.9, significant at the .001 level of confidence.

Clearly, then, the Massachusetts data indicate that career-bound superintendents more frequently than place-bound superintendents receive a mandate from the employing school board. Moreover, a small sample of Illinois superintendents confirms the finding.[6] Deprin asked ten superintendents: "Did the board set any particular goals that they wanted you to accomplish?" Answers from the men, who all had relatively short tenure, were placed in three categories by Deprin: (1) clearly defined, easily recalled expectations, (2) very general, difficultly recalled expectations, and (3) no expectations. Four of the five career-bound men gave responses in the first category, and one in the second category. Among the five place-bound superintendents, three were scored in the third category and one in each of the other two categories. Again, career-bound men áre more likely to receive a mandate. Ranking the categories as indicated above and applying a Mann-Whitney U test produces a z value of 2.02, significant at the .04 level of confidence.

When a career-bound man enters into discussion with a school board prior to being offered the position, a distinct give and take occurs between him and the board. The board indicates that all is not well and that there is a desire to right the situation. Usually the board does not specify what needs to be done, but only what is wrong. Both directly and indirectly the career-bound man receives a mandate to act. The tone of the preliminary meeting indicates the board is saying "we want you." Such a situation enables the career-bound candidate to make known his demands. As one career-bound superintendent warmed up to the discussion of his working relationship with the school board, he said:

> You see, when they brought me in they had certain things they wanted to do which they discussed with me. And I told them frankly that I had certain things that I wanted to do, too, because I was in no trouble—I had a job that was about as good as this one. I felt that I was entitled to make some deals at the time, too, so I told them certain things that I wanted to be able to recommend on

---

[6] See Louis D. Deprin, "Superintendent Succession and Administrative Patterns" (Ph.D. diss., University of Arizona, 1965), p. 64. This is a secondary analysis of his data.

and we had a very good understanding and we never had any trouble with the board as to policies and as to my place in the scheme of things.

By taking someone from outside the containing organization and giving him a mandate, the board signals a desire for a break with old ways. In this sense the board commits itself. Thus it must go along with the career-bound man and give him the backing needed to carry out the mandate. More than one school board president has said that he viewed his *sole* function during the career-bound superintendent's first year as that of supporting the new man.

With the place-bound man, the initial relationship with the board is quite different. No clear mandate comes from the board. The usually brief discussion with the potential superintendent is carried out with the board saying in effect: "Here it is, you can have it." It is as if the man were inheriting the superintendency. It is not a matter of "Do you want it and if so under what conditions?" or "We want you," but simply, "Here it is." In such a setting no bargaining occurs. All discussion is based on the assumption that the man wants the job. Because the board has not discussed pressing problems or given a mandate to act, it is not self-conscious about supporting the place-bound superintendent.

The mandate gives the career-bound superintendent ample support from the board. There is another factor in his favor. Everything about him is not known; and favorable assumptions are made about his ability as an administrator. He is assumed to be of extraordinary quality until he proves otherwise. This is not the case with the place-bound man; his limitations and strengths are public knowledge.

In addition, many superintendents interviewed realize career-bound men receive more support from the school board than do place-bound men. Most frequently the examples cited involved personnel problems. For example:

> When appointments are involved the insider often takes a back seat. He is not given freedom. The board and the general public are more apt to accuse him of self-interest. He has friends and cronies and people will say he's interested in building their salaries up. He has to give more justification for his moves.

One superintendent, who had first-hand knowledge of support given the two types, made some very instructive comments. As a career-bound man he had held two superintendencies for a total of 12 years. After resigning to work full time on a doctor's degree, he accepted an assistant superintendency in mid-year in a district where the superintendent was hospitalized and not expected to live. The understanding was that the new man would be made the superintendent. But the superintendent recovered and held his post for five more years. After he had been in the district five and one-half years, the replacement was elected superintendent. Toward the end of his second year in the superintendency he made the following comments:

> ... actually, you might say I'm in my second [four-year] term right now, because the people knew me and I became involved in a great number of community activities during the first years I was here.

(Does that make any difference?)

> Well, frankly, I would have preferred to come in directly from outside. I would have preferred to take over at the end of the first year I was here. I think that it's very desirable to have a year or a part of a year on the job, prior to taking over, in that it becomes so much easier for you to have a picture of the whole school system. ... When it comes to going on as it did for me, then you're old before you get started.

(What do you mean?)

> Well, as far as the general public is concerned you've been here five years. The new superintendent—I'll have to admit that I think some of the esteem of the new superintendent is lost when you've been in the district for five years before taking over the superintendency.

(What difference does it make?)

> Changes are harder to make. I think they wonder why you weren't more successful in getting changes if this were desirable—why weren't you able to affect it while you were assistant, for example. These people will wonder—well, if this was a desirable change, why weren't you able to convince your predecessor that it was a desirable change?
>
> You know, I frankly believe that I could have got more done if I had come in fresh with the school board. Now, I'm not inferring that they don't back me, but it's been my experience that a new man taking over a job—in other words, I'll have to say something maybe *four* times now to get the punch in because they were used to me before I even took over the superintendency. But a new man —the very first time you come out with something new they're going to think about it more critically, and take it with a little more sincerity, I believe, than they would this way. They get accustomed to the individual, seeing him around and talking with him. . . .

Thus the importance of the conditions under which the two types are employed and the mandate or its absence take on added meaning and are reflected in the performance in office of the two types.

SALARY

School boards, when faced with the opportunity or problem of replacing a superintendent, can elevate someone from within to the post or bring someone in from outside the containing organization. It has been shown that promotion from within occurs only when the board is satisfied with the way the schools have been administered and that when a board is dissatisfied, the new superintendent is brought in from outside the containing organization. Further, it has been shown that because the man from outside, the career-bound superintendent, is often hired when a state of dissatisfaction exists, he is given a mandate by the board. No such mandate is given the man from within, the place-bound superintendent, for he is called upon only when the schools have been judged to be running smoothly.

In selecting a new school superintendent, the school board has a relatively free hand. The board also has a relatively free hand in determining what it should pay its new superintendent. Differences in the commitments of the two kinds of superintendents and in the conditions under which they are hired, plus the fact that only the career-bound man is given a mandate, suggest that the two types will be rewarded differently. The place-bound superintendent's commitments to the school system and the community are obvious. He apparently is more interested in making a career in the particular school system than in making a career as a superintendent. Thus he probably demands less for his services than a career-bound superintendent and is paid less. It is instructive to note that in a sample of 745 superintendents, 38 responded positively to the comment that a willingness to accept the salary was a reason for being selected for the superintendency they now held. In the sample, 9 per cent of the place-bound men, as opposed to 3 per cent of the career-bound men, made this acknowledgment. (The difference is significant at the .001 level of confidence.[7])

Regarding salary paid, it is clear that career-bound superintendents are the favored type. Table 6–5 shows the mean first or second year salary paid the two types of superintendents by school system size. Note

---

[7] AASA, *Profile of the School Superintendent.* This is a secondary analysis of the raw data.

Table 6–5

SALARIES OF 1st OR 2nd YEAR SUPERINTENDENTS

POPULATION OF DISTRICT	MEAN SALARY OF PLACE-BOUND SUPERINTENDENTS (Number)	MEAN SALARY OF CAREER-BOUND SUPERINTENDENTS (Number)	DIFFERENCE
500,000 and over	$19,750 (2)	$22,250 (1)	$2,500
100,000 to 499,999	14,200 (7)	19,200 (8)	5,000
30,000 to 99,999	12,400 (14)	15,000 (15)	2,600
10,000 to 29,999	10,300 (9)	11,500 (42)	1,200
5,000 to 9,999	9,450 (5)	10,450 (21)	1,000
2,500 to 4,999	6,900 (3)	8,100 (15)	1,200

Source: Secondary analysis of data in AASA, *Profile of the School Superintendent.*

that career-bound superintendents command from $1,000 to $5,000 more a year than place-bound superintendents when beginning salaries are considered. Further, the place-bound superintendent never catches up. A difference in salary favors career-bound superintendents regardless of time in office.

7

Performance in Office: Successors and Their Policies

Thus far in the consideration of the natural history of the succession cycle of school superintendents, it has been shown that the two main types of successors can be distinguished by their actions prior to taking office. They differ in terms of their origin with relation to the containing organization and this, in turn, is reflected in different commitments to place of employment and commitments to the career. Further, it has been shown that the two types exhibit different career styles and achieve different positions in the social structure of school superintendents. And, as the preceding chapter has shown, the two types are hired under different circumstances: place-bound men are hired only when satisfaction exists among school board members about the performance of the school system; and only career-bound superintendents are hired when the performance of the school system has been deemed to be unsatisfactory by the school board.

This chapter and the following two move to another stage in the history of the succession cycle. They center on the performance in the superintendency of career- and place-bound superintendents. The actions of the two types in the superintendency are analyzed together and comparisons of their performance are made regarding policies, working relationships with school personnel, and adoption of educational innovations. Thus, against a background of explicit differences between the two types, a knowledge of the differing conditions under which they are employed, attention to performance in office shows how career- and place-bound superintendents lead their containing organizations down different courses.

PREOCCUPATION WITH RULES

School superintendents, new to a particular position, tend to be preoccupied with rules and rule-making early in their stay in office.[1] They are not alone. Such a pattern has been reported about successors in at least two other settings. For example, Grusky observed in a prison camp:

> The new supervisor, confronted with a role in which he had had no previous experience . . . responded by formalizing relationships in the organization. The most important changes which he instituted involved the substitution of formal rules for informal ones. After being in charge of the camp for about a month, he inaugurated a list of 52 rules that the inmates were instructed to abide by rigorously. . . . Hand in hand with this policy went an increasing emphasis on closer supervision and stronger security controls. Policies which were consistent with the ideology of custody quickly supplanted the earlier pattern. . . .[2]

A similar observation about a successor in an industrial firm was made by Gouldner. He quotes the firm's labor relations director saying: "*New* managers always tend to rely more on the rules. They call up and ask us if we have a list of rules they can use."[3]

THE FUNCTIONAL SIGNIFICANCE OF RULES

Because successors in several settings have been reported to cause a surge in rules, it seems appropriate to inquire into the functional signifi-

---

[1] The term *rule* is used in a broad way to include such items as definition of work day, procedures for handling paper, and people and policy statements.

[2] Oscar Grusky, "Role Conflict in Organization: A Study of Prison Camp Officials," *Administrative Science Quarterly*, Vol. 3 (March, 1959), 464.

[3] Alvin W. Gouldner, *Patterns of Industrial Bureaucracy* (Glencoe, Ill.: The Free Press, 1954), p. 94.

cance of rule making for the individual successor, and to raise the question of why successors become preoccupied with rules.

A successor has needs which rule making fulfill. One important need seems to be to create the impression that he is busily engaged in vital organizational activities. This impression seems universally difficult for successors to maintain. School superintendents report that at first they have time on their hands; they do not quite know what to do. This is a common feeling that goes with a new job. The making of rules thus becomes functional; it occupies time, it is highly visible and produces a definite product, and it is easy to engage in even with only limited detailed knowledge about the organization. Because of his limited knowledge, the successor cannot enter into certain activities. Consequently he postpones these in favor of rule making, which enables him to maintain, at least to some degree, the impression that he is productively engaged with the organization.

A second need involves the identity of the successor. Although speaking of individuals in small, informal groups, Schutz's comments about the need to establish identity are meaningful:

> The inclusion phase begins with the formation of the group. When people are confronted with one another they first find the place where they fit . . . and see if one is going to be paid attention to and not be left behind or ignored. . . . He is asking "Will they know who I am and what I can do, or will I be distinguishable from many others." [4]

These feelings and questions preoccupy successors. As a result, the common notion develops that "all new bosses should fire someone during the first week," and that new office furniture and decorations are imperative. Acts of this order are functional for they help force people to the realization that a new man is on the scene. For example, in one of the school districts under study a superintendent moved his office when he took over the position. In his words:

> The old superintendent occupied what is the center office and people learned over a period of time not to go in there. They called it the "black-out" room because the only light was the one over the desk and it was kept quite dark. He was ill for the last several years and never made any decisions so there wasn't any use for people going to see him. Much of the work was done by the secre-

---

[4] William C. Schutz, *Firo: A Three Dimensional Theory of Interpersonal Behavior* (New York: Rinehart and Company, 1958), p. 169.

tary. People would stop in to raise questions with her. That's why my desk is out here [face to face with the secretary]. I want to be where I can see people.

After a year and a half on the job, the superintendent moved into what became a well-lighted "black-out room."

Rule making also helps to establish the identity of a successor. His new rules clearly signal that a new man has arrived and that things are going to be different. They also give the successor a chance to see if people are going to pay attention to him. Rules are accepted or ignored, thus giving the successor an idea of the extent of his "inclusion."

A successor with plans also has a need to know about the probable reaction of the organization to change. A new superintendent needs to know how sensitive the school system is to change, how much it will strive to keep things as they are. Also, he must have some idea where his support lies, and where the resistance is likely to be the greatest. Rule making is functional for the successor with this need. A new rule or renewed support of an old one elicits reactions, becomes a topic for casual conversation, and a basis for speculation about the successor. The successor can use it as a "goblet issue." [5] With it he can come to learn who's who, their commitments, and the readiness of the system for change. A new rule may be of little importance and may not even be an integral part of the successor's plan, but it can serve a vital need for him.

Rule making, then, fulfills at least three needs of successors: it conveys the impression that he is busily engaged in vital organizational matters, it gives him an identity, and it gives him the means of knowing who's who and the degree of readiness of the system for change.[6]

The rule-making activities of one career-bound successor illustrate some aspects of this need fulfillment process. Some months prior to taking office a newly elected superintendent listed in a newspaper interview several changes he expected to make in the school system. One specific change concerned the curriculum time schedule. The newspaper story, with its statement of contemplated change, was received with mixed emotions by the staff members. But it did make everyone

---

[5] "The term is taken from an analogy to a cocktail party where people sometimes pick up their cocktail glass, or goblet, and figuratively use it to peer through to size up the other people at the party. Goblet issues are those which, in themselves, are of minor importance to the group members but which function as vehicles for getting to know people." *Ibid.*, p. 170.

[6] Gouldner indicated that the successor under his observation made rules because he did not have informal lines of influence. *Patterns of Industrial Bureaucracy*, pp. 84–85.

aware of the impending reign and indicated that some thought had been given to the system. It also caused speculation as to how successfully these changes might be made and about what else might be forthcoming for the school system.

Before taking office the superintendent received eleven letters, eight of which were signed. The announced changes had served as goblet issues; they were reasons for writing the letters and vehicles for discussing things of greater importance that the individuals wished to convey to the successor. Through the letters, the superintendent obtained some preliminary ideas as to people's identities, their commitments, and their support.

After the successor took office, one person became a self-appointed reporter of staff reactions to the contemplated changes. The reporting did not identify individuals, but simply mentioned types of reactions, their popularity, and their generalized location. This person was recognized by others as one who could "get the superintendent's ear." But some staff members suggested that much of what the self-appointed reporter relayed was "manufactured," and these observations reached the superintendent.

Seven months after assuming the office, the superintendent issued a bulletin outlining his new curriculum time schedule. The superintendent realized the near impossibility of enforcing such a schedule, and he did not regard the new rule as crucial. It is important to note, however, that the curriculum time schedule rule was functional for his needs as a successor. By means of reactions to it he later filled, from within, two important new positions on the administrative staff and came to understand who stood where and for what. He was able to make some changes easily and to reconsider knowingly or postpone making others.

The Rise and Fall of Bureaucracy

One of the basic points in the classic definition of bureaucracy is that all activities are governed by rules. In this sense, the operation of a bureaucratic organization depends on a file of rules. The proposition that rule making is functional for successors is suggestive of an aspect of bureaucratization of an organization.

What is suggested is that rule making in an organization will not proceed at a steady pace, but will be marked by surges and declines. As the successor continues in office his preoccupation with rules declines, but not because all activities run smoothly or because he runs out of rules. It is just that the successor no longer has a need to make rules. They have served a purpose, and now the superintendent can assert that it is better to operate without rules, because you can get trapped in your own rules.

The "rule" history of an organization relates to the "succession" history. What an organization experiences in the cycle of succession of chief executive officials is a rise and fall of bureaucracy. Four pieces of evidence support this proposition. The first was stated in terms of the functional significance of rule making for individual successors.

The second comes from the almost universal difference noted between the old and the new superintendent by those close to the position. Quite simply, the difference is frequently stated this way: "The new superintendent's organized."

A secondary analysis of a study by Melvin Seeman provides the third piece of supporting evidence. Seeman's study contains scores that indicate the superintendent's "behavior in delineating the relationship between himself and members of the work group, and in endeavoring to establish well-defined patterns of organization, channels of communication, and methods of procedure."[7] This trait is called "Initiating Structure."

The results of a secondary analysis of the relationship between the "Initiating Structure" trait as perceived by staff members and the length of time in office of the individual superintendents is shown in Table 7–1.

Table 7–1

INITIATING STRUCTURE SCORES

TIME AFTER SUCCESSION	NUMBER OF SUPERINTENDENTS	MEAN INITIATING STRUCTURE SCORES
1st and 2nd years	13	39.1
3rd and 4th years	7	37.7
5th and 6th years	9	37.8
7th and 8th years	6	37.3
9 years and more	15	37.8

Source: Secondary analysis of raw data from Melvin Seeman, "Social Mobility and Administrative Behavior," *American Sociological Review*, Vol. 23 (December, 1958), 633–42.

---

[7] Melvin Seeman, "Social Mobility and Administrative Behavior," *American Sociological Review*, Vol. 23 (December, 1958), 634. Detailed information about the scale can be found in Andrew W. Halpin, *The Leadership Behavior of School Superintendents* (Columbus, Ohio: The Ohio State University Press, 1956).

The mean "Initiating Structure" score for the sample of 50 superintendents was approximately 38 and the standard deviation was about 4.5. The higher the score, the more the superintendent "delineated the relationship between himself and members of the work group, and . . . established well defined patterns of organization, channels of communication, and methods of procedure." Though the differences are small, the figures show that the successor at first "runs a taut ship," but later loosens up.

The fourth piece of evidence is the most compelling. It is a count of the number of rules ten school superintendents made, year by year, during their first four years in office. Over the four years the ten superintendents made 496 rules: 171 in the first year in office, 179 in the second year, 68 in the third year, and 60 in the fourth year.[8] About three times as many rules were made by the superintendents during their first two years in office as were made in their second two years in office.

The rule-making history of an organization thus can be seen as related to the succession cycle. Men new to the particular executive post set high rule production records, but as time passes, rule making becomes less functional for them and their rule production record significantly diminishes.

TYPES OF RULES AND THE ORIGIN OF SUCCESSOR

Although new superintendents tend to be preoccupied with rules, their preoccupation takes on varied forms which can be correlated with the origin of the successor. Place-bound superintendents concentrate on old rules. Publicizing and reinforcing old rules and assessing the extent to which they were being taken into account are two of their activities. Their preoccupation with rules does not include a reassessment of rules or any extended work with new rules. They tend to tighten existing rules rather than to alter or redefine either the internal commitments or the external ties of the school system. On the other hand, career-bound superintendents devote most of their rule-making activities to orders that fill in gaps or supplant old ones. They do modify and redefine the commitments of the school systems.

Both types of successors develop new rules, but career-bound men do so more frequently. In a sample of five of each kind of superintendent,

---

[8] Source: Secondary analysis of data contained in Deprin, "Superintendent Succession and Administrative Patterns," pp. 76, 80.

the career-bound men exhibited a mean of about 45 rules in the first two years in office and the place-bound men exhibited a mean of about 29 rules over the same time period.[9] Moreover, a difference existed between new rules made by the two types. When the place-bound superintendent formulated a new rule, it typically related to the technical or managerial aspects of the systems. The following are examples: "All individuals responsible for making classroom observations will turn in a weekly report stating the number of such observations and follow-up conferences." "Decisions regarding promotion in questionable cases will be made by the child's teacher, the building principal, the elementary supervisor and the home and school visitor." Career-bound superintendents also made new rules in the technical and managerial aspects of the school. But career-bound superintendents were more prone to make new rules at the institutional level of the organization; that is, rules that go beyond technical and managerial concerns and modify or change the character of the organization and its relation to the environment. Examples of this kind of new rule are the establishment and integration of a kindergarten and the employment of school social workers to serve the school in relating individual pupils with the law, the courts, welfare agencies, and psychiatrists.

A further difference in the rule-making activities of the two types relates to the restrictive or liberalizing nature of the rules. Deprin examined 496 rules made by ten superintendents during their first four years in office with this question in mind: "Are those affected by the rule able to make more or fewer decisions as a result of the rule?"

If the rule, in his judgment, permitted more decisions to be made by those affected, he called it a liberalizing rule; if it did not, he called it a restrictive rule. He found in his small sample that about 78 per cent of the rules made by career-bound superintendents and about 24 per cent of the rules made by place-bound superintendents were "liberalizing rules."[10]

Rules formalize internal and external commitments of an organization and are instrumental in establishing its course and character. The rule-making activities of career- and place-bound superintendents are generally in keeping with the conditions of their employment. Place-bound men, hired only when the state of affairs has been defined as satisfactory, make rules that tend to reflect an effort to perpetuate that state of affairs. In contrast, place-bound superintendents make fewer rules; thus they change the management of the school system less, make fewer

---

[9] *Ibid.*
[10] *Ibid.*

rules which relate the school system to its environment, and tend to keep a tighter rein in that their rules usually restrict the decision making of those affected.

Differential Rule Vulnerability

Although functional for successors, rules cannot "shape up" all sectors of a public school system. Rules are potentially damaging to an individual regarding his formal status, his work, method of his work, and his responsibility and chain of command relationships. Some sectors of public schools have more vulnerability to the potential damage from them. Rules pose no threat to the formal status of classroom teachers; they are at the bottom of the professional hierarchy. Their status can only be improved. Although it is easy to make rules about what classroom teachers should do and the way in which it should be done, it is practically impossible to enforce such rules. Surveillance is impossible. Teachers work in closed rooms and they can be observed only with difficulty. In addition, teachers can make a strong claim for professional autonomy. They are under the direct supervision of a principal who stands between them and higher school authorities. Thus because the principal intervenes between the teacher and the superintendent, it is possible to corrupt the authority and rules of the superintendent. This does not mean, however, that rules cannot harass teachers. Taken together, these factors suggest that classroom teachers are relatively invulnerable to damage from rules; thus it is difficult to gain obedience from or influence them by the use of rules.

However, school administrators—particularly the central office staff— are vulnerable to damage from rules. They can be demoted to the classroom or to some lower level administrative position. Their position in the chain of command can be altered to their dissatisfaction. In addition, administrators are few in number, and they work in the open and in one geographic location. Thus surveillance can be quite effective. They can make no claim for professional autonomy. Further, rules can alter the administrator's work and routine. Reporting directly to the superintendent eliminates the possibility of corruption of authority. Thus through the use of rules it is easier to gain obedience from administrators because they are more vulnerable to damage. Because rules can be effectively employed to "control" or secure obedience from administrators, but not from classroom teachers, an incoming superintendent who wants to influence all sectors of the school system must establish different authority relationships for teachers and for administrators.

Impression Management: A Case Study [11]

Differential rule vulnerability poses a serious problem of influence for the superintendent who sees himself as an agent of change. For dynamic changes to be effective, he must receive support from the teachers. He must also recognize that change does not occur simply by making rules and trying to enforce them, or by announcing changes on paper and assuming they have been put into operation.

In this connection the actions of one of the career-bound superintendents observed are instructive. This superintendent saw himself as a change agent; in fact, he was selected on a wave of reform. Concerned about dynamic changes in the system and aware of the need for diffuse support throughout the organization, the superintendent approached teachers and central office administrators differently in an effort to gain the support he wanted.

He attempted to establish an authority system with teachers based on personal ties or on loyalty to him and his purpose. At the first meeting with his teachers he stressed that the aims, goals, and purposes of administration and classroom teaching are identical. This idea was basic to the maintenance of the front with teachers, but it was supported by several conspicuous activities. He seized opportunities to build personal ties with the teachers; if a teacher was ill for more than a day or was hospitalized, the superintendent made a visit to the home or hospital. He responded appropriately to significant events such as births, deaths, or honors. His staff was instructed to keep him informed of such events. On the frequent occasions when he had errands that took him into the various school buildings, he was totally occupied trying to remember names, being seen, saying the right thing, and building personal ties.

His attention to teachers' welfare paid off in a fund of good will which was helpful in building personal ties. He pushed through a fringe benefit program, established a new method of determining sick leave which benefited teachers, created a short-term, emergency-leave pro-

---

[11] Phrases or terms such as *impression management, front,* and *presents himself,* though they call up many interpretations, are used here in the neutral sense in which Goffman has used them. To set the stage for the use of the terms, he said: "The perspective employed in this report is that of the theatrical performance; the principles derived are dramaturgical ones. I shall consider the way in which the individual in ordinary work situations presents himself and his activity to others, the way in which he guides and controls the impression they form of him, and the kinds of things he may and may not do while sustaining his performance before them." Erving Goffman, *The Presentation of Self in Everyday Life* (Garden City, N.Y.: Doubleday & Company, Inc., 1959), p. xi.

gram, and announced that the first (rather than the last) item on the budget to be fixed would be teachers' salaries. Through these activities, he won the consent of the teachers' organization to be its representative in bargaining with the school board for higher salaries and fringe benefits. Some teachers, lamenting their loss of direct contact with the school board, felt that they would suffer in the long run; but most felt, however, that there was no need for concern now that "he's on our side."

Another element in impression management with teachers concerned the way bad news was handled. If a particular job needed to be done or a piece of information had to be conveyed that was not in keeping with the impression the superintendent was attempting to maintain, he did not request the job or convey the information; a subordinate did.

The superintendent presented a different front and managed a different impression to his central-office administrative staff. With them he was impersonal, not particularistic, showed little concern about their out-of-school lives, and exhibited little warmth for their in-school lives. To them he seemed all business. One subordinate remarked:

> _____ has never once asked "How's your family?" To me this is like saying "hello" particularly when you work together day after day, but he never does it. He's kind of impersonal. . . . I have made quite a revision in procedure of obtaining substitutes. When I presented the plan to _____, he didn't say "It's a good job" or "It's a bad job," he simply accepted it. He has never commented about my work. The only thing I ever heard was one time he spent about five minutes telling the board what a tremendous job I was doing and how pleased he was with the new system.

Similar comments were made by other central-office administrators. With staff administrators, support was tied to performance; with teachers, support was secured on a personal basis. The superintendent acted universalistically with staff administrators and particularistically with teachers.

This is not to say that the superintendent could not influence or gain obedience from the central-administrative staff; obedience does not depend on a personal tie. Instead, it depends on a system of rules and procedures which govern activities and serve as the basis of the authority relationship. The front the superintendent manages with the staff administrators was one of rationality, which contrasts sharply to the front maintained with the teachers.

The superintendent's success in maintaining these two different impressions is documented by the teachers' and central office administrators' description of him. Twenty words, gleaned from casual conversations about the superintendent, were presented in alphabetical order to the nine members of the central office administrative staff. They were instructed to check ten words that best described the superintendent. Thus from among the twenty words, the administrative staff made ninety choices. The same list and instructions was mailed to a ten per cent random sample of teachers employed in the system. Thirty-four usable questionnaires were returned. This gave the teachers 340 choices. The choices of the two groups are shown in Table 7–2.

Table 7–2

**WORDS CHOSEN BY TEACHERS AND ADMINISTRATORS
TO DESCRIBE THEIR SUPERINTENDENT**

WORD	PERCENTAGE OF TEACHER RESPONSES	PERCENTAGE OF ADMINISTRATIVE STAFF RESPONSES
Appreciative	9%	2%
Considerate	6	2
Cooperative	9	4
Courageous	5	6
Devoted	7	10
Kind	6	1
Professional	9	2
Sympathetic	9	1
Thoughtful	7	2
Understanding	9	2
Subtotal	76%	32%
Efficient	3%	4%
Fair	3	7
Impersonal	1	4
Organized	4	10
Orderly	2	10
Precise	3	4
Predictable	2	9
Rational	2	6
Strict	0	3
Systematic	2	7
Subtotal	22%	64%

The table shows the words—not as presented to the respondents—divided into two groups. The words at the top of the table suggest personal or particularistic attachment or ties to the superintendent, and the words at the bottom suggest universalistic ties of perception of the superintendent as simply a capable executive.

The two fronts managed by the superintendent were effective: about three-fourths of the words selected by teachers and about one-third of the words selected by the staff administrators were in the "personal" category; and about one-fourth of the words selected by the teachers and about two-thirds of the words selected by the staff administrators were in the "executive" category.

The way this superintendent related to teachers and staff administrators indicates that the word choices of the two groups were neither accidental nor simply reflective of different kinds of opportunities to view the superintendent. Instead, they reflect the way the superintendent presented himself to the two different groups.[12] He was aware of the two fronts he was managing. He could, and did, talk about the front with teachers, but was unable to relate this to the front with staff administrators. He looked upon his relationship with staff administrators with a what-else-do-you-do attitude.

The points that need underlining in this analysis are: (1) The superintendent was intent on "shaping up" the school system and providing a better quality of service to the pupils. (2) To make the changes envisioned, support was needed from all those who would put the changes into operation. (3) Influence over staff administrators, but not over classroom teachers, could be gained by the use of rules. Classroom teachers are not vulnerable to damage from rules; change depends on their cooperation and cannot be obtained by issuing rules. Another means of access and control must be utilized. (4) The successful management of two fronts, one with teachers which attempted to establish personal ties and one with the staff administrators which attempted to establish rational or legal ties, was functionally significant for the superintendent because it enabled him to influence all important sectors of the school system. This influence, in turn, permitted some progress toward his goal of change.

The authority systems this superintendent attempted to maintain resemble two of the three ideal types of authority—rational-legal, traditional, and charismatic—described by Max Weber.[13] Rational-legal authority rests on a system of rules and a belief in their legality. Obe-

---

[12] The instrument was used in another district with another superintendent, but no pattern was formed by the responses of teachers and central office administrators.

[13] Max Weber, *The Theory of Social and Economic Organization*, trans. A. M. Henderson and Talcott Parsons (Glencoe, Ill.: The Free Press, 1947), pp. 328ff.

dience on the part of an individual responding to a rational-legal authority system results from "his capacity as a member of the corporate group and what he obeys, is only 'the law' " [14] and "insofar as they obey a person in authority, [they] do not owe obedience to him as an individual but to the impersonal order." [15] This type of authority best characterizes the superintendent's relationship to the central office administrative staff.

On the other hand, the authority relationship with the classroom teachers was charismatic, for it rested on "devotion" to the specific character of an individual person and the cause. Under such an authority system, the "leader is always in some sense a revolutionary, setting himself in conscious opposition to some established aspects of the society in which he works." [16] And those who obey are "actuated by enthusiasm for the 'cause' and by personal loyalty to the leader or both." [17]

Many students of organizations make an implicit assumption that a single kind of authority relationship holds for everyone in all sectors of an organization at any one time. But two exceptions occur. Robert Dubin has written "in most organizational situations there is likely to be more than one type of authority present at the same time." [18] However, he does not present data to support the statement. And his explanation that "the different kinds of authority may be called into play under varying conditions in which the organization is operating" [19] is not particularly satisfying.

Dubin does go on to suggest that in a position that spans many organizations, a person may utilize all types of authority, and that Franklin D. Roosevelt exercised charismatic authority over many New Dealers and part of the electorate, traditional authority over the armed forces, and rational-legal authority over the governmental bureaus. As the other exception, Janowitz has said: "But it is the sources from which military authority derives power and influence that are of crucial consequences. Does authority flow from custom, law, or the personal characteristics of a key officer, to mention the categories of analysis offered by Max Weber? Of course, no hierarchical organization of any size or

---

[14] *Ibid.*, p. 330.
[15] *Ibid.*, p. 330.
[16] *Ibid.*, p. 64.
[17] *Ibid.*, p. 65.
[18] Robert Dubin, *Human Relations in Administration* (New York: Prentice-Hall, Inc., 1951), p. 198.
[19] *Ibid.*, p. 198.

complexity has its authority system based on a single principle." [20] Janowitz develops a case: "The impact of technology has forced a shift in the practices of military authority. Military authority must shift from reliance on practices based on domination to a wider utilization of manipulation." [21] He asserts "the transformation of military authority can be seen in every phase of organizational behavior—for example, the narrowing of the differences in privileges, status, and even uniforms of the enlisted man and the officer, the development of conference techniques of command from the smallest unit to the Joint Chiefs of Staff themselves." [22] What Janowitz has said is that one type of authority system might be appropriate at one time but not at another, and authority systems shift over time. In a similar fashion Weber has pointed out that charismatic authority is unstable and that it becomes transformed into traditional or rational-legal authority. [23]

The analysis of the superintendent's behavior indicates that within an organization where change is desired there may be a need to simultaneously maintain two types of authority systems; and that the formal structure of the organization, the nature of the personnel, and their differential rule vulnerability may be the causative factors. [24]

An explanation of why the superintendent attempted to maintain a charismatic authority system with the classroom teachers has been offered, but there remains the question of why he attempted to maintain a rational-legal rather than a charismatic authority system with the central office administrative staff. Several parts of a full explanation suggest themselves. Undoubtedly the contrasting ways he presented himself enabled the teachers to identify with him and see him as being on their side and separate from the administration system in general.

---

[20] Morris Janowitz, *Sociology and the Military Establishment* (New York: Russell Sage Foundation, 1959), p. 25.

[21] *Ibid.*, p. 38.

[22] *Ibid.*, p. 40.

[23] Max Weber, *Social and Economic Organization*, pp. 66, 363ff.

[24] Speaking of change in a mental hospital, John and Elaine Cumming report: "A great deal of our effort was spent in persuading the old guard that things *could* be done. They found it hard to accept the idea that a routine could be changed without dire consequences. Besides this traditionalism, the poverty of the environment and the poor communication system had frustrated them so often in the past that their skepticism was profound. They considered it impossible that each patient have his own clothes when the lockers were broken; the lockers could not be fixed because the tinsmith had refused once before to fix them. At this juncture it was vital for us to ensure that the tinsmith fix the lockers and, in general, to exercise leadership having a shade of 'charisma,' in order to overcome the inertia of the staff." Milton Greenblatt, *et al.* (ed.), *The Patient and the Mental Hospital* (Glencoe, Ill.: The Free Press, 1957), p. 60.

Further, given the circumstances of the staff administrators, a rational-legal authority system could quite easily be established; of more importance, once established, its maintenance "costs" are not nearly so great as the costs of the continual need to reinforce and maintain a charismatic authority system. Finally, it seems relevant that "human relations" training has been encouraged and applied at the point where managers meet workers and not where workers meet managers.

IMPRESSION MANAGEMENT AND SUCCESSORS: IMPLICATIONS FOR ORGANIZATIONAL DEVELOPMENT

That executive succession has potential developmental significance for an organization can hardly be questioned. But for significant developments to occur, support must be forthcoming from the important sectors of the organization; in public schools, support is necessary from administrators and teachers. The way one superintendent attempted to manage the situation suggests some important differences between place-bound and career-bound superintendents and significant development of the school system.

The career-bound man is in a better position to gain initial support from the teachers than is the place-bound man. The man from outside comes in unknown and, so to speak, has a new lease on life.[25] Being unknown, he can gain influence over the teachers unfettered by their intimate knowledge of his past performance. He may not have ready-made friends, but neither does he have built-in enemies. Thus his performance is not shaped by friendship and animosities.

The man promoted from within the containing organization was known before and thus is less able to manage something approaching a charismatic front. Because of past activities, he undoubtedly has supporters and nonsupporters. He cannot start anew with them. Thus the place-bound superintendent starts with divided support and the constraining influence of a heritage of personal relationships in the organization.

It is difficult for the man from within to establish that he is on the teacher's side. Some of his past activities plus his long history of being

---

[25] The popularity of role playing in the training of teachers and administrators undoubtedly gives opportunity to study the possibilities in "getting a new lease on life." And articles such as "How to Choose a Leadership Pattern," *Harvard Business Review*, Vol. 36 (March–April, 1958), 95–100, by Robert Tannenbaum and W. H. Schmidt suggest indeed that one might profitably think about how to present himself in a leadership position given the chance to start again.

on the administrative staff make this so. Right or wrong, he is almost always seen as the school board's man. His lack of bargaining power with the board is understood both by teachers and the board; and it is expected that because he wants to maintain his job, he will not antagonize the board members.

Because of the low rule-vulnerability of classroom teachers, the superintendent must establish some unorthodox authority system with them or default in the authority relationship. This second choice has some attraction. The superintendent who defaults can indicate that teachers are identified with the cause of education. He can say that sufficient clues to obedience and action are based on and come from indoctrination by and identification with the teaching profession. Thus he will say that teachers are in good hands, and he can safely default. But by defaulting the superintendent indicates that his behavior is not consequential in gaining influence over teachers. Such a default has consequences for the development of the system. In such a school system, then, development or improvement depends on impetus coming from the teaching profession.

The place-bound superintendents observed in the case studies defaulted in the authority relationship with the classroom teachers; they acted almost as if teachers did not exist. If the place-bound man does attempt dynamic changes, he does so from a point of weakness. First he must face the constraining influence of his friends and enemies in the organization. Then he must understand that the conditions under which he was hired indicate that change is not necessarily wanted nor expected from him; and if change is proposed, all sorts of questions are raised.

The rule-making and support-gaining activities of career-bound and place-bound successors, then, give some indication of the way they relate to their containing organizations. With respect to organizational development, place-bound superintendents tend to tighten what exists as they function during the first few years in office; the career-bound superintendents, through the introduction of new rules, attempt to alter the direction the school system is moving. In addition, the constraints on the two types as they attempt to gain influence over the organizational course are unequal; clearly, the career-bound superintendent has the advantage. Those promoted from within are handicapped by a heritage of established relationships within the school system which constrains them in the making of new rules and limits them in seeking support for administrative actions. Career-bound superintendents, lacking a heritage of established relationships, are not constrained. They have greater flexibility in rule making and allied moves directed at gaining support.

8

Performance in Office: Successors and Their Staff

School superintendencies frequently change hands. One survey reports that one out of five superintendents is new to his position each fall; [1] another states that the mean length of time in office is about nine years. [2] This does not mean, however, that the replacement of the superintendent is unimportant. With succession comes a sense of excitement, apprehension and expectation. It is an event that calls forward an array of feelings from school personnel. Some see it as an opportunity; others as a threat.

RECEPTION

The reception given a newly appointed superintendent by the staff he inherits can include courting, indifference, or a wait-and-see attitude, resentment, and resistance. Would-be administrators and those administrators who feel misplaced in the hierarchy and not understood or fully appreciated by

[1] E. E. Mosier and J. E. Baker, "Midwest Superintendents on the Move," *Nation's Schools*, Vol. 49 (January, 1952), 44–46.

[2] AASA, *Profile of the School Superintendent*, p. 81.

the organization typically engage in courting. "Courters" do not feel that their commitment to the school system is reciprocated. If the successor comes from outside, *he* is the target of the wooing. If he comes from inside, the wooer concentrates not only on the successor, but all those who stand in his favor.

Employees whose commitment to the organization is deemed reciprocated and who stand relatively untouchable or immune to the acts of the successor generally take a wait-and-see position. This group is mostly composed of teachers and noncertified or service employees.

Resentment and retrenchment usually come from those with a high stake in the organization who can anticipate alteration in their job security. Those with a high commitment to the organization which has been reciprocated, but who are susceptible to the acts of the successor, may be resentful of his arrival and retrench as a preliminary step to resistance. Most administrative personnel are in this group.

Of high importance is the change that occurs to the general social system of the organization as the successor takes over. Change-over is a natural time for reasserting old needs and presenting new ones to the incoming superintendent. Thus succession often triggers a change in the status quo. Succession, then, provides the impetus for individuals, particularly those on the administrative staff, to reassess their position in the informal organization of the school system.

With succession the informal power system can be drastically altered. Greater fragmentation or consolidation of interest groups within the organization may result from change in the chief executive official; such change may also lead either to abandonment of old alliances and the formation of new ones or to the solidification of present alliances.

What happens within the social system of a school district as it takes on a new superintendent partly depends on the origin of the successor. Extended observations in the four school districts revealed that in the case of career-bound superintendents, the temporary result is a solidification of informal relationships *within* hierarchical levels; that is, with the coming of a new man from outside, interaction increases *among* elementary school principals, central office administrators, and others in similar groups, but decreases *between* elementary principals and central office administrators, and so on.

Evidence of this phenomenon is largely historical and impressionistic. A "we" feeling is apparent within hierarchical groups; however, it was reported to heighten with succession. By far the most telling evidence is that elementary school principals in one district gathered for an evening of card playing for the first time when a career-bound man took over the superintendency. Reportedly the real purpose of the card game was to enable the principals to discuss their common interests and to determine how they related to the new superintendent.

Thus individuals within a hierarchical level, becoming self-conscious about their common identity, begin to concentrate on the notion that they indeed have something in common worth protecting. They ignore —at least temporarily—their differences and past rifts and act as if an alliance might best serve their purposes.[3]

Thus neutrality and peace reign within hierarchical levels. Succession from outside acts as a catalyst to weld together strong units within hierarchical levels capable of unified action. This means that such units could be mobilized easily to thwart the successor's plans. But such a unit also could act in a unified way to promote and develop the changes introduced by the successor, or components of the unit could drift apart and renew old alliances. The course taken by these self-conscious units is dependent upon an array of factors, but it is important to realize that with the succession from outside, there develop strong neutral units within hierarchical levels which the successor has a possibility of utilizing as he comes to terms with the organization.

The situation differs, however, when a man from inside moves into the office of superintendent; no such neutral units within hierarchical levels develop. Succession from inside seldom alters the social systems of the districts observed. Of course some individuals move to positions of greater power and influence and some are cut back, but this movement is an extension of a trend. Where solidification of informal relationships takes place it is *across* hierarchical levels rather than *within* them. Individuals within hierarchical levels do not feel self-conscious about their common identity, and old rifts and interest group lines are neither temporarily forgotten or altered.

Thus the two types of superintendents face distinctly different social systems within their containing organizations; the man from within faces a structured social system, and the man from outside faces a social

---

[3] This kind of alliance has been called a *horizontal defensive clique* by Melville Dalton and is reported to arise with a crisis. His observations of clique activities lead him to state: "Usually this clique is strong for only the limited time necessary to defeat or adjust to a threat. Since nothing is served by its persisting longer, it lapses to dormancy until another crisis, but when active it forces the symbiotic [vertical] cliques into quiescence. However, it is inherently weak because of the vertical breaks likely to occur from action by resurgent symbiotic cliques. That is, as a horizontal structure the clique is made up of department segments, each restrained temporarily by the chief's preoccupation with interdepartmental action." *Men Who Manage* (New York: John Wiley & Sons, Inc., 1959), p. 61. Reprinted with permission from Melville Dalton, *Men Who Manage*, 1959, John Wiley & Sons, Inc.

system which has been temporarily suspended because of his arrival. The internal political structure and interest groups go largely undisturbed when a place-bound man takes over. In a sense he is like an army officer taking command when the battle rages, when the lines are drawn, and when individuals and groups are committed to courses of action. Because the conflict goes on undisturbed by his arrival, his maneuverability and ability to reshape the conflict and its lines are limited. At least for the time being he must follow the army.

As the career-bound superintendent takes over, however, the existing social system becomes suspended. People identify with one another on an organizational rather than on a personal basis. The career-bound superintendent takes command between skirmishes or during a temporary truce. Thus he has a chance to reshape the conflict. Because the place-bound man faces a structured and the career-bound man faces a temporarily suspended social system, the latter has a distinct advantage regarding organizational development and adaptation.

An indication of the state of the social system of school personnel after succession is revealed in findings about organizational climate reported by Hall. He administered Halpin and Crofts' "Organizational Climate Description Questionnaire" to school personnel in 28 elementary school systems. While he found no significant relationships between the origin of the successor and scores on the eight subtests or six organizational climates, he found that the superintendent's origin plus his term in office were significantly related to the organizational climate. Based on his work, Hall concluded: "The most desirable (most open) working relationships appear to be developed within the staffs of schools in districts administered by superintendents who are Outsiders [career-bound] of Short Tenure. The least desirable (most closed) tend to develop in districts administered by Insiders [place-bound] of Short Tenure." [4]

EXPANSION OF THE ADMINISTRATIVE STAFF

The "propensity of all organizations to expand" has been cited by Barnard,[5] and by Terrien and Mills, who also note that the administra-

---

[4] Clarence L. Hall, "Relations of Origin and Tenure of Superintendents to the Organizational Climate and Adaptability of Schools." (Ph.D. diss., Stanford University, 1966), 106.

[5] Chester I. Barnard, *The Functions of the Executives* (Cambridge, Mass.: Harvard University Press, 1938), p. 159.

tive component constitutes a larger and larger per cent of all those employed in the organization.[6] The administrative hierarchy obviously expands in relationship to some potentially identifiable variable. Change in leadership appears to be a variable significantly related to expansion of the administrative hierarchy. A recent example of this variable was provided by Pope John XXIII, who increased the number of Cardinals from 52 to 75 within 13 days after taking office.

The need for loyalty seems to be the connecting link between new leadership and expansion of the administrative hierarchy. The new chief executive, more than his predecessor, squarely faces the problem of loyalty and of building goals into the social structure of the organization. As Willard Waller observed,

> ... the carryover of old loyalties is one of the most difficult things the new executive has to face. Sometimes the teachers who still preserve the memory of the former superintendent band themselves together in order to handicap the new executive; such fights are usually carried over into the community at large, and they often become very bitter. . . . The opposite situation to the above is that of the person succeeding a man who has left many enemies in the community. The enemies of the former superintendent . . . attach themselves at once to the new superintendent, as if determined to prove that they are not trouble-makers, that it is possible for this new man to get along with them, and that it therefore should have been possible for his predecessor to do so.[7]

The genuine and general nature of the problem of transferability of loyalties makes it commonplace to see old organizations abandoned or bypassed and new ones created to handle marked changes in orientation and goal. The Franklin D. Roosevelt administration and Carlson's Raiders of World War II and elements of the 1965 Elementary, Secondary School Act provide concrete examples of this practice. The fear is that the old agency or organization, which embodies precedents for action, alliances, and personal loyalties, can muster resistance capable of drastically restricting the full development of a new program. But often, even though new goals are sought or weak ones emphasized, the

---

[6] F. W. Terrien and D. L. Mills, "The Effect of Changing Size Upon the Internal Structure of Organization," *American Sociological Review*, Vol. 20 (February, 1955), 11–13.

[7] Willard Waller, *The Sociology of Teaching* (New York: John Wiley & Sons, Inc., 1932), pp. 96, 99. Reprinted with permission from Willard Waller, *The Sociology of Teaching*, 1932, John Wiley & Sons, Inc.

organization cannot be cast aside; it must be maintained. When this is the case, as with public schools, the alternatives are to oust people, bring in new ones, or both.

Loyalty is especially vital at a time of organizational change. For change to be realized, loyalty and commitment to an idea or a person must be diffused extensively throughout the organization; certainly it must be forthcoming from key positions. At a time of change, loyalty enhances the possibility of satisfaction of crucial organizational needs such as stability of lines of authority and communication, stability of informal relations within the organization, and homogeneity of outlook with respect to the meaning and role of the organization.[8] Further, as Michels has observed:

> In proportion as the chiefs become detached from the mass they show themselves more and more inclined, when gaps in their own ranks have to be filled, to effect this, not by way of popular election, but by cooptation, and also to increase their own effectives wherever possible, by creating new posts upon their own initiative. There arises in the leaders a tendency to isolate themselves, to form a sort of cartel, and to surround themselves, as it were, with a wall, within which they will admit those only who are of their own way of thinking ... leaders do all in their power to fill up gaps in their own ranks directly or indirectly by the exercise of their own volition.[9]

The place-bound superintendent has less need to give direct attention to loyalty. His heritage of relationships within the school system undoubtedly involves loyalty to him by some staff members. This loyalty may be sufficient, for the conditions of employment indicate he is not going to change the school system in any dynamic fashion; in fact, his rule-making activities tend to make this very clear. On the other hand, the career-bound successor has a real need to give direct attention to loyalty. Success for him tends to be defined as change; and as has been shown, his rule-making activities tend to be more oriented toward change. This mandate for change, coupled with the lack of ready-made support, makes it clear that he has reason to retool the organization.

This reasoning underlies two propositions about successors and ex-

---

[8] These are among the organization needs identified by Philip Selznick. See "Foundations of the Theory of Organization," *American Sociological Review*, Vol. 13 (February, 1948), 25–35.

[9] Robert Michels, *Political Parties: A Sociological Study of the Oligarchical Tendencies of Modern Democracy* (New York: The Free Press, 1962), p. 126.

pansion of the administrative staff. The first proposition is that during the early stages of the succession cycle, the number of outside successors who add to their central office administrative staff will be greater than the number of inside successors who add to their central office administrative staff.[10] To test the proposition the succession and staffing histories of the 100 largest school districts in California were gathered for the period from 1952 to 1956. The size of the central office administrative staff inherited by a new superintendent was compared with the size of the staff two years later. The central office administrative staff was taken as the index because its size is less responsive to increases in numbers of pupils and, therefore, more responsive to the wishes of the superintendent than is the size of the total administrative staff. If the pupil enrollment of a district is growing, as it was in all of these districts, the system must provide additional administrative personnel to operate new schools built to accommodate the increased enrollment. There is little choice in the matter; the new schools must have principals. But even if a district adds new buildings, it is not compelled to add certified administrative staff at the central office level. Such additions involve choice.

Thus in a district where there are new buildings completed, the matter of adding to the total administrative staff is, so to speak, out of the superintendent's hands. But when an addition is made to the central office administrative staff, such an addition is directly related to the discretion of the superintendent.

In the 100 districts, 35 superintendents were new to their posts during the 1952–1956 period. Twelve of them were place-bound. Three of the 12 place-bound and 14 of the 23 career-bound superintendents increased the size of their central office administrative staff during their first two years in office.

The statistical significance of the difference is beyond the .05 level of confidence [11] and, therefore, the proposition that during the early stages of the succession cycle the number of career-bound successsors who

---

[10] A somewhat similar, but untested, proposition to the effect that an outsider as a top executive will utilize an "assistant-to" more frequently than an inside top executive has been advanced by T. L. Whisler. See "The 'Assistant-to' in Four Administrative Settings," *Administrative Science Quarterly*, Vol. 5 (September, 1960), 209. Gouldner noted, in his study of one outside successor, the process of expansion of the administrative staff and its relation to the needs of the successor. In addition he pointed out the process of strategic replacement as an alternate procedure in meeting the successor's needs. *Patterns of Industrial Bureaucracy*, pp. 88–91.

[11] This difference and all more extreme cases in the distribution of those who added to the staff and those who did not yielded a probability of .024 on a one-tailed test using the Fisher Exact Probability Test.

add to their central office staff will be greater than the number of place-bound successors who add to their central office staff can be accepted.

This proposition is based on the assumption that expansion of the administrative hierarchy involves discretion and that it is not directly tied to the rate of enrollment growth. The assumption is rendered acceptable if school districts identical in size and in the pattern they exhibit in enrollment growth do not exhibit an identical pattern in the making of additions to the central office administrative staff. This assumption can be tested by comparing the number of additions made to the central office staffs over a specified time in school systems of identical size and rate of growth, but operating under different conditions which logically might bear on the discretionary act.

The second proposition relating to successors and expansion of the administrative staff is concerned with the successor's impact on the rate positions are added to the administrative staff. The proposition has two parts: (1) during the early stages of the succession cycle, career-bound successors will add more positions to the central office administrative staff than will "old" superintendents in comparable districts during the same time span; (2) the converse applies for place-bound successors.

Each of the 35 sample districts with new superintendents was paired with another district if the following conditions were met: (1) type of district was the same (*i.e.*, elementary, high school, unified), and the size and pupil-growth figures corresponded year by year for the relevant time span with less than a difference of 10 per cent of the enrollment of the district and (2) the superintendent had been in office at least four years and was therefore "old." Four districts were lost from the sample because these conditions could not be met. If more than one district met the conditions from the total population of the 100 largest districts, the "twin" was drawn at random from among those in the qualifying group. Eleven districts with place-bound successors and twenty districts with career-bound successors could be matched with a "twin."

The eleven districts with new place-bound superintendents added a total of five positions at the central office level, an average of .45 positions per district within two years after the succession. Their twin districts with old superintendents added fourteen such positions, an average of 1.27 positions per district over the same time span. The twenty districts with new career-bound superintendents added 39 positions, an average of 1.9 positions per district within two years of the succession, and their twin districts with old superintendents added 25 positions, an average of 1.25 positions per district over the same time.

Both of the differences are statistically significant beyond the .01 level of confidence.[12]

Three marked trends stand out. Career-bound superintendents are more prone to add to the central office administrative staff during the first few years in office than are place-bound superintendents. Moreover, career-bound men add to the staff at a faster pace during the first few years in office than do superintendents in general in comparable school systems; and place-bound men add to the central office administrative staff at a slower rate during the first few years in office than do superintendents in general in comparable school systems.[13]

But what happens to the rates after the first two years in office? An explanation is needed, for if the rates of making additions to the staff continued, obviously the central office staffs of districts with place-bound superintendents would become significantly smaller than central office staffs of districts with career-bound superintendents.

Ultimately, two possibilities arise. Over time the two types create a similar number of new positions, but at different times throughout the succession cycle. Given the needs of the career-bound superintendent, it is possible that he creates the new positions all at once and early in his stay in office. The place-bound superintendent, however, does not create new positions all at once, but spreads them out over his term in office.

The second possibility is that over time the two types do not create a similar number of new central office administrative positions. It may be that because of the conditions of employment and commitments of the two types of successors and the head start of the career-bound man, the place-bound man will never catch up with him in creating new staff positions. The expansion rates of each of the types may converge toward a mean as time goes on; but still, this would mean that there would be a difference between the number of positions added over time in similar districts. This explanation further implies that a growing school district reduces the difference between the size of its central

---

[12] The Wilicoxon Matched-Pairs Signed-Ranks Test was used.

[13] Additional data in general support of these findings is reported by Deprin. In a sample of ten superintendents, five of each type, he found that during the first four years in office the career-bound men added a total of twenty-six positions to the central office administrative staff, and the place-bound men added a total of four such positions in the same time period. See Deprin, "Superintendent Succession and Administrative Patterns," p.82.

In addition to noting that career-bound men increase the size of staff by expanding the central office administrative force, Deprin also reports that career-bound superintendents tend to increase the ratio of professional staff to students and that place-bound men do not. (pp. 94–97.)

office staff and the mean size for comparable districts when replacing a place-bound man with a career-bound man and the other way around. These explanations remain speculative, however, for data are lacking.

The successor does not have full authority to add people to his administrative staff; the school board is the sole agent authorized to hire personnel for the public schools. In addition, it has control of expenditures. Nevertheless, in most instances where additions have been made, it is because of the effort of the superintendent rather than the board. There are probably two factors at work which should be called on to explain fully the differences in addition to the administrative staff by the two types. The primary factor, covered in the discussion above, is the career-bound superintendent's greater need for loyalty on two grounds; one that he lacks a history in the district which could provide some ready-made loyalty, and the other that he is going to make changes in the system and, therefore, has a greater need for loyalty. This indicates that the *need* to make additions is not balanced between the two types; neither is the *ability*. Thus the secondary factor is that, as already indicated, the career-bound superintendent receives more support from the school board than does the place-bound superintendent. Even if he wanted to, the place-bound superintendent would have more difficulty in increasing his staff because he lacks sufficient support from the board.

A career-bound superintendent's autobiography adds evidence that enlarging the administrative staff is a repetitive response of a career-bound superintendent in most of the school districts where he might find himself.

> My greatest regret in leaving Passaic was that I should be without the help of Miss Catherine Bryce, who had there become so successful in her supervisory work. . . . Naturally I was hoping that in Newton there would be need of just such services as she was so competent to render. I soon found the need to be even much greater than I had dared hope. My recommendation of her appointment . . . to begin with the opening of the next year, was unanimously approved by the School Committee . . .[14]
>
> . . . The group which I found already on the ground [in Minneapolis] was soon increased and strengthened by several new appointments. Among the new appointees deserving of special mention, in evidence of the strengthening of the headquarters staff, were Miss

---

[14] Frank E. Spaulding, *School Superintendent in Action* (Rindge, N.H.: The Richard R. Smith Co., Inc., 1955), p. 251.

Catherine T. Bryce, coming from ten years' experience in the schools of Newton, Massachusetts, and Dr. H. Lester Smith . . .[15]

In view of the fact that, on their own initiative, the Board [in Cleveland] was giving me a much publicized 'free hand'. . . it seemed to me essential to reach agreement at once respecting certain appointments and reappointments to the professional staff. . . .

To discharge efficiently my unprecedented administrative responsibilities, I must have competent, reliable, and loyal assistants . . .[16]

According to my plan of organization, which was unanimously approved by the Board [in Cleveland], there would be a Deputy Superintendent in general charge of the senior and junior high schools. . . . Assisting the Deputy Superintendent would be two Assistant Superintendents . . .

In general charge of the kindergarten and elementary grades would be an Assistant Superintendent, who would have as supervisory assistants four General Supervisors and a Supervisor of kindergartens . . .

First to fill the position of Deputy Superintendent was Robinson Godfrey ("G.") Jones, called from the superintendency at Rockford, Illinois. Associated with him as Assistant Superintendents were A. C. Eldredge, reappointed, and F. E. Clark, well prepared by ten years' experience as high school teacher and Principal and Superintendent of Schools.

In general charge of the kindergarten and first six grades was Assistant Superintendent Catherine T. Bryce, called from a like position in Minneapolis. Associated with her as General Supervisors were Jessie D. Pullen and Florence A. Hungerford, both reappointed; Eva T. Seabrook, brought from an elementary school principalship in Passaic, New Jersey, to which she had been appointed on my recommendation; and Olive G. Carson, from a teaching position in Newton, Massachusetts, to which she had also been appointed on my recommendation.[17]

The fact that a position was created for Miss Bryce in four systems, plus the appointments mentioned in the last paragraph, indicate that taking on this superintendent also meant asuming an obligation to his extended professional "family."

What kinds of individuals, then, would a superintendent, performing as a change agent, add to his administrative staff? Obviously, he will want subordinates who would provide (1) stability of informal relations within the organization, (2) stability of lines of authority and

---

[15] *Ibid.,* p. 471.
[16] *Ibid.,* p. 540.
[17] *Ibid.,* p. 553.

communication, and (3) homogeneity of outlook with respect to the meaning and role of the organization.

The superintendent could enlarge his administrative hierarchy by promoting from within or by bringing them in from outside. If he chooses the latter method, he can get employees well known or relatively unknown to himself. These characteristics of individuals would have little consequences for the organizational need of stability of lines of authority and communication.

If the need is for simple loyalty, employees seemingly could be obtained in sufficient number simply by awarding them with an administrative position. This would not insure the superintendent that he was getting stability of informal relations or homogeneity of outlook. To enhance the possibility of stable informal relations within the organization, the superintendent would seemingly place someone from within the school system in the newly created position. In this way he could get someone on his team who might be influential in the balance of informal relations. An outsider could not be expected to figure immediately in the stability of informal relations. The crucial factor regarding homogeneity of outlook seems to be that the superintendent must be quite familiar with the thinking of an individual added to the staff. This undoubtedly means he needs someone whom he has worked with in the past or someone with whom he has had some fairly extensive professional association.

The career-bound superintendent, obligated to improve the school system but lacking a heritage of social relations in the district, seemingly has more reason to be concerned with loyalty to him and his plans than does the place-bound man. This need for loyalty from personnel, added to the necessity of changing the system, is reflected in the way the two types of superintendents apply varying practices of expanding the administrative staff. Loyalty to the superintendent might be built into the organization as the superintendent creates new administrative posts and picks occupants to fill them.

But expansion of the administrative staff is only one of the ways an executive may choose to build a loyal following among the staff he inherits. He can also re-assign administrative personnel. If a superintendent chooses this alternative, he can place those most loyal to him and his plans in central or key positions and shuffle others to the side lines. By upgrading some, he seemingly can secure commitments and understanding from them. Obviously, then, career-bound superintendents, more than their counterparts, would re-assign administrative personnel. Although the evidence comes from a very small sample, this is indeed the case. Among a sample of ten superintendents, five of each type,

Deprin reports that re-assignment of administrative personnel was exercised nine times as often by career-bound men as it was by place-bound men new to the office.[18]

MANAGEMENT OF INTERNAL INTEREST GROUPS

The need for stability of informal relations always is important to an organization. People bring their own personalities with them into organizations, and in the course of trying to satisfy their own psychological needs and adhering to their own values they spill over the neat boundaries prescribed by the formal organization. Consequently, informal relations cannot be ignored in the analysis of organizations, even though such attention should not be expected to explain and account for everything.

Although informal relations are important to the functioning of an organization, their effect on the organization is debatable. Informal relations within an organization serve many purposes. Several research studies report that the informal organization "serves the very significant role of providing a *channel of circumvention* of the formal prescribed rules and methods of procedure," [19] bolsters the formal organization by strengthening "the motivation for the fulfillment of substantive prescriptions and commands issued by the official agents of the corporate body," [20] and restricts goal attainment of the organization in that "systematic 'soldiering' is group activity." [21] The most noticeable feature of the literature on informal organization is the agreement about its impact. Some sample statements indicate that "informal organizations exist as a necessary condition for collaboration," [22] or "formal organizations are vitalized and conditioned by informal organization." [23]

All of this raises the neglected question of the extent to which an organization is consciously able to draw upon and shape this great resource and the processes or strategies involved? My purpose here is

---

[18] See Deprin, "Superintendent Succession and Administrative Patterns," 84–86.

[19] Charles H. Page, "Bureaucracy's Other Face," *Social Forces,* Vol. 25 (October, 1946), 10.

[20] Edward Shils, "Primary Groups in the American Army," *Continuities in Social Research: Studies in the Scope and Method of "The American Soldier,"* Robert Merton, *et al.* (eds.) (Glencoe, Ill.: The Free Press, 1950), p. 22.

[21] Donald Roy, "Quota Restriction and Goldbricking in a Machine Shop," *American Journal of Sociology,* Vol. 57 (March, 1952), 427.

[22] F. J. Roethlisberger and W. J. Dickson, *Management and the Worker* (Cambridge, Mass.: Harvard University Press, 1939), p. 562.

[23] Barnard, *Functions of the Executive,* p. 120.

simply to look at an aspect of this larger question by considering courses of action open to school superintendents as they attempt to work with informal relations that take the form of an interest group perceived to be detrimental to the purpose and functioning of the school system.[24]

Of course the superintendent labors with constraints on his relationship to the informal organization. For one thing, he lacks the means of direct influence on the interest group through participation in it as a member, especially if it is dedicated to countering his programs. It is paradoxical that while informal organization is a primary force in an organization, the chief executive official has little influence or directive power over it. A place in the informal organization requires interaction denied the executive because his status keeps him at arm's length, and the informal organization, by its nature, keeps apart from him. Thus the actions of an administrator regarding internal interest groups are restricted to manipulation from outside the organizational body. This is not to say that he has no influence, but simply that his influence is not direct.

For example, during the observation of the four successors, there were three attempts by superintendents to influence internal interest groups. The first instance, involving Williams, an arithmetic supervisor, and Rodgers, the director of the elementary school program, has an important history. Williams had a long tenure in the position; most of the time he was the only administrative person between the superintendent and teachers at the individual school level.

As the district grew, Rodgers was hired as an associate superintendent in charge of the elementary schools. He was given the assignment with instructions to "keep hands off the arithmetic program and supervision of it." Upon the retirement of the superintendent, Rodgers moved into the top position. At the time, the central office administrative staff included the superintendent, Rodgers, Williams and his assistant, a director of the elementary program, and two other persons. In spite of the size of the administrative force and the existence of a position which logically should be responsible for the whole elementary

---

[24] This is not to mean that all actions are planned. An example of the unplanned variety is the replacement of prisoners by civil service employees in many quasi-administrative positions in prisons—positions in which incumbents could grant to, or withhold, important privileges from prisoners. Such action disrupted the informal organization of the prisoners in that it pulled the rug out from under old power positions which had played an imposing part in the social system. Hartung and Floch suggest that this action largely accounted for the wave of prison riots of a few years ago. See "A Social-Psychological Analysis of Prison Riots: An Hypothesis," *Journal of Criminal Law, Criminology and Police Science,* Vol. 47 (May–June, 1956), 51–57.

program, Williams reported directly to the superintendent. He had no responsibility links with the director of the elementary program. Both the old superintendent and Rodgers were friends of Williams, who came from a prominent family in the community.

A few months before the superintendent retired, efforts were made to organize the administrative structure. Williams' position in the formal structure was changed; he was to report to the director of the elementary program. The latter reportedly made consistent efforts to establish some working relationship with Williams and his assistant, but did not succeed. Williams operated as if no change in authority relations had been made, and the superintendent permitted him to do so. Faced with this and other problems, the director left the system.

At this point Rodgers took over the superintendency. He took three steps to put the arithmetic supervisor into place. First, he stopped social contacts with Williams. This was done with some difficulty and regret for he valued Williams as a friend. Second, he asked an outside agency to conduct a survey of the educational program of the district; he was assured by the agency that its report would recommend that Williams report to the director of the elementary program and that a change be considered in the arithmetic program and its supervision. The final survey report contained clear statements on both counts. Third, he prepared job descriptions for all central office personnel. These described the authority relationship between the arithmetic supervisor and the director of the elementary program.

These efforts met with limited success because Rodgers' long-time relationships in the social organization of the school system interfered. When a conflict developed between Williams and the new director of the elementary program, all actions, positions taken, and positions not taken were interpreted with consideration for the past power of Williams and the past social friendship of Rodgers and Williams. Thus the steps taken by Rodgers were unsuccessful because of his previous relationships. He could dismiss the past, but those who knew him could not.

The second problem with an internal interest group involved conflict of a different nature. This time the interest group was the teachers' organization. Toward the end of a place-bound man's first year in the superintendency, the teachers' organization underwent a self-initiated revival. Five persons were responsible for the new nature of the organization with its increased power.

A principal vacancy occurred during the year, and people both inside and outside the district sought the position. The president of the teachers' organizations was given the principalship although he would not receive full credentials for such a position until he spent one more summer session at the university. In spite of the precedent that administrators do not take a part in the teachers' organization, the new principal served out his term as president. In administrative staff meetings, the new principal had a special role in relation to teachers. When an agenda item involved teachers, all heads turned to the new principal for his reactions and suggestions; he served as the authority. After he spoke, the discussion usually ended.

By promoting this classroom teacher to a principalship, the superintendent absorbed into the administrative framework the leader of a group antagonistic toward the administration. Such an act may be called *cooptation,* "the process of absorbing new elements into the leadership or policy-determining structure of an organization as a means of averting threats to its stability of existence.[25] This concept has played a significant part in the analysis of adaptative responses of organizations to meet the need for security in relation to social forces in the organizational environment. Cooptation might be seen as an adaptative response in meeting another need of organizations, the need for some stability of informal relations within the organization. Here the threat is not to existence but to power, control, and harmony. Each time an administrative group has a chance to fill an administrative position it has an opportunity to exert some influence on the informal balance of power and control within the organization and to take a hand in setting the situation regarding internal harmony.

Not all promotions to administrative positions involve cooptation. The following conditions are suggested as defining cooptation *within* an organization:

1. Within the organization exists a group or groups on whom the organization depends and with whom it must deal in real matters. A union is such a group. But even in the nonunion shop, if there is a group which can influence action in a substantial and enduring way, this group qualifies. The group must represent a source of power within the organization, but it can be formally or informally organized. Further, it is not necessary that the group be at the worker level; cooptation can take place between various levels of management.

2. The person involved in cooptation must be more than a member of the group: he must be influential, informed, or both. His position must be such that he has something to offer.

3. There must be attempt to employ the person, at least to deny

---

[25] Philip Selznick, *TVA and the Grass Roots* (Berkeley, Calif.: The University of California Press, 1949), p. 13.

the group its established leader. The person might also provide information on sentiments which would put management in a more protected spot, exert influence on the interest group by the direct contact of the individual, and exert influence without direct contact, as when an interest group might feel that if their "representative" had a hand in the development of a program, it must be worthwhile. The hiring of the president of the teachers' organization as principal, then, qualifies as cooptation because the three conditions were present.

A third instance of an attempt to manage an internal interest group struggle involved the administrative staffs of two high schools. The schools, through their principals, had a history of uncooperativeness when the new superintendent took over. The struggles between the two principals, and among their subordinate administrators were, in the view of the superintendent, costly to the district. No improvement could be made to one building without a corresponding improvement to the other. Both schools were fiercely independent about the use of books and supplies; and as the district grew, there were successful and unsuccessful attempts at gerrymandering attendance boundaries to secure athletes and desirable students.

The career-bound successor, after becoming familiar with the situation, decided he was in no position to enter into the conflict himself, that it would do neither him nor the school system any good. No one in the district, in his judgment, had enough influence with both groups to work out the struggle. Thus he resorted to a procedure most often called *democratic* administration; that is, he created a committee of the high school principals and some of their staff, gave them the broad outlines of an agenda, met with them until they established a chairman, and received progress reports from them. In a way he simply created an environment in which the interest group struggle might be resolved. My observation period ended too soon for a report of the final outcome, but headway was being made and points of conflict were being resolved.

In summary, it has been suggested that a chief executive cannot exert a direct, powerful influence in the management of internal interest group struggles. He cannot act from within the group; he can only operate around the edges. At least three courses of action are open to him:

1. He can call on outside sources to apply some neutral influence. In the case reported, this took the form of a school survey. A citizen's committee also might serve this purpose.

2. The most drastic action is aimed at changing the structure of the informal group and through it the informal organization. This calls for

realigning the membership. It can be accomplished by promotion, demotion, reassignment, or dismissal. An informal group may be perceived as having damaging aims. Because a group often is most vulnerable through its leadership, an effective means of disorganizing the group (at least temporarily) is to remove its leader. The leader may be removed from the total organizational group, or he may be taken into the administrative group where it is hoped that he can be saved; that is, in time, he will yield to the in-group and adopt a new ideology. Another practice that fits this category is that of placing a person with the desired ideology in the physical setting of the group with the hope of changing its structure through his entry and later mobilizing its resources into prescribed channels. All actions aimed at changing the structure of the informal group rest on administrative knowledge of present group structure.

3. Another course of action is less direct and serves two purposes. One purpose is to make the organization more human, to mold the organization to the needs of the human tools. The other purpose is to exert influence on the natural relationship between the formal and informal aspects of organization. Granting autonomy, encouraging participation in decision making, and using committee procedures in problem solving or policy formation fits this type of action and are part and parcel of the rubric "democratic administration." Granting autonomy, for example, is clearly making the organization human, but it is also acting on the natural relationship by sanctioning the informal organization's strain to shape the direction of the organization. Participation in decision making and committee procedures invite the informal organization to act officially in setting the course of the organizational group and providing an environment favorable to the solution of internal interest group struggles. Further, they give the administrator a chance to hear the thinking of the informal organization and to attempt to modify that thinking by exposure to and involvement in administrative matters.

The Successor's Program and Counteracting Forces

The propositions examined thus far have shed some light on the differences between place-bound and career-bound school superintendents. Any full understanding of the ways these two types relate to their containing organizations must include a tracing out of the responses of organizations to the successors. The chief executive official is not the whole organization. Though highly influential, he is not the complete master of the organizational course. Much is known about counteracting forces within organizations undergoing change, change that is frequently initiated by career-bound successors. Under conditions of change counteracting forces have been expected and have been traced out in case studies.[26]

When the new leadership is committed to system maintenance, as place-bound superintendents are, the tracing out of counteracting forces has been ignored. There is no reason to expect, however, that counteracting forces are not present both when leadership is committed to change and when it is committed to maintenance of the system. We might expect, however, that under the two unlike conditions the counteracting forces would take on different forms and come from different quarters of the organization and its environment.

The lack of this kind of material cannot be corrected here. My purpose is simply to raise the question of counteracting forces to leadership bent on system maintenance and to relate an observation made in the four school systems.

For example, place-bound successors may be unwilling to press for advances in salary and welfare benefits for teachers. The salary of a place-bound superintendent is not so far removed from teachers' salaries that he feels pressure to bring teachers' salaries into line. Also, some judge school systems by how much they pay teachers. To raise teachers' salaries may be a side payment bargained for and won by career-bound superintendents, but not by place-bound superintendents. Furthermore, place-bound men may know the teachers too well to be concerned over their salaries. In contrast, the career-bound man knows only the salary figures for the district; and if salaries reflect unfavorably, he will raise them without thought of teachers as individuals.

This may have been the basis of teacher resentment in one system observed. In one of the systems with a place-bound superintendent, the teachers' organization took a more aggressive attitude than customary regarding salaries and welfare benefits. The teachers' organization assumed that to gain welfare benefits and salary increases it must work around the superintendent (which was contrary to past procedure) and deal directly with the school board. Members of the teachers' organization felt the superintendent would not fairly represent their case. He was disturbed. The development established a precedent and a new definition of the relationship between teachers, superintendent,

---

[26] As samples of this kind of material, see S. M. Lipset, *Agrarian Socialism* (Berkeley, Calif.: University of California Press, 1950), and Gouldner, *Patterns of Industrial Bureaucracy.*

and school board with possible far-reaching consequences. The consequences of the precedent, however, could not be adequately assessed during the time given to this research.

By way of a summary with respect to organizational development, the material in this chapter about the way the two types relate to their staff has unearthed several differences that give some further indication of the different courses career-bound and place-bound superintendents move their organizations. One point is that with a place-bound man coming into the superintendency, the social system of the district goes unaltered; but with an outside successor the social system becomes suspended. This gives the career-bound man greater flexibility and latitude in altering the lines of internal conflict and in presenting a case for support. Secondly, the career-bound superintendent, but not his counterpart, retools the organization for a different course of action by adding to the administrative staff and re-assigning administrative personnel. Finally, it has been shown how it is possible for the heritage of relationships belonging to a place-bound superintendent to hamper his actions in attempting to manage detrimental internal interest group struggles.

9

Performance in Office: Successors and Adoption of Educational Innovations

School systems are self-conscious about their significant purposes. They exist in a rapidly developing culture where knowledge and technological advances pressure them to seek change in their educational practices. Adoption of new educational practices is just one means by which school systems attempt to adjust to their environment. The educational enterprise also changes its structure, size, and support; alters its definition of purpose or mission; and adjusts the number, competencies, and characteristics of its personnel. But the adoption of new educational practices—practices which alter the instructional program—seems to be at the center of the issue as school systems attempt to provide adequate education for their clients.

In this chapter, as in the preceding two, attention is on the performance of the two types of superintendents. Here we want to see if career- and place-bound superintendents perform differently in meeting the challenge or problem of adoption of educational innovations. Before we can examine the performance of the two kinds of superintendents, a case must be made to show that superintendents and their actions play a major role in the adoption of educational innovations.

On one level, to support the notion that school superin-

tendents play an important role in the adoption process, there are assertions made by students of the process, such as the following made
by Brickell based on his story of the change process in school systems
in New York State:

> New types of instructional programs are introduced by admin-
> istrators. Contrary to general opinon, teachers are not change
> agents for instructional innovations of major scope. Implication: To
> disseminate new types of instructional programs, it will be neces-
> sary to convince administrators of their value.
>
> Instructional changes which call for significant new ways of
> using professional talent, drawing upon instructional resources, allo-
> cating physical facilities, scheduling instructional time or altering
> physical space . . . depend almost exclusively upon administrative
> initiative. . . .
>
> [The superintendent] may not be—and frequently is not—the
> original source of interest in a new type of program, but unless he
> gives it his attention and actively promotes its use, it will not come
> into being.[1]

In addition to assertions that portray the superintendent as a central
figure in the process of adopting educational innovations, research
exists that demonstrates the power and utility of variables attached to
the superintendent for predicting the rate at which school systems
adopt educational innovations.[2]

Perhaps the most widely spread notion, however, about adoption of
educational innovations involves the overriding importance of money,
or expenditure level of the school system. In summarizing the findings
of the many studies of adoption of educational innovations carried on
by Paul Mort and his students, Donald H. Ross said: "If but one question can be asked, on the basis of the response to which a prediction
of adaptability [adoption of innovations] is to be made, the question
is: How much is spent per pupil?[3] This conclusion accurately repre-
sents the Mort studies, but it should be noted that they dealt almost
exclusively with financial matters. Thus, it comes as no surprise that
a review of studies dealing almost exclusively with the relation of

---

[1] Henry M. Brickell, *Organizing New York State for Educational Change* (Al-
bany, N.Y.: State Department of Education, 1961), pp. 22–24.

[2] See Richard O. Carlson, *Adoption of Educational Innovations* (Eugene, Oreg.:
Center for the Advanced Study of Educational Administration, 1965), and James
A. Reynolds, "Innovation Related to Administrative Tenure, Succession and Orienta-
tion" (Ph.D. diss., Washington University, 1965).

[3] *Administration for Adaptability* (New York: Metropolitan School Study Council,
Teachers College, Columbia University, 1958), p. 15.

money to rates of adoption of educational innovations concludes that money is of overriding importance. In a far more broadly conceived examination of rates of adoption of educational innovations, Reynolds reports a low correlation between expenditure level and rate of adoption and further states:

> A fundamental assumption of the study was that the superintendent is significant in determining the adoption of new practices. While this assumption was not tested directly as a hypothesis, it is made tenable by the fact that certain hypotheses based upon this assumption were supported by the data. Also, the three factors identified as relating significantly to innovation . . . were all attached to the superintendent. Of the four variables which were not related to the superintendent (number of teachers, tax rate, expenditure level, and assessed valuation), none made an important contribution in explaining the variance in innovation when attributes of the superintendent were controlled.[4]

The empirical evidence and the assertions clearly suggest that the school superintendent is neither a victim of a local budget nor a powerless bureaucrat; to the contrary, they suggest that he is an important influence in the adoption process.

Adoption Rates

The use of modern math was first introduced into Allegheny County in 1958; by 1963 it had been adopted by over 80 per cent of the school districts. Table 9–1 shows the cumulative percentage of adoption of modern math by the two types of superintendents year by year from the time of its introduction until 1963, among the 43 superintendents who were in their position from at least 1957 on and, therefore, had an equal opportunity in the time sense to adopt the practice.

Several features of the table are noteworthy. Modern math was first accepted by a career-bound superintendent, and over one-fifth of the career-bound men adopted the innovation before it was adopted by a place-bound superintendent. By 1960 about one-half of the career-bound superintendents had adopted modern math, compared to 20 per cent of the place-bound men. A smiliar cumulative percentage dif-

---

[4] Reynolds, "Innovation Related to Administrative Tenure, Succession, and Orientation," p. 96.

A similar conclusion regarding expenditure level was reached by Carlson. See Carlson, *Adoption of Educational Innovations*, pp. 61–63.

Table 9–1

RATE OF ADOPTION OF MODERN MATH AND
TYPE OF SUPERINTENDENT

Year of Adoption	Career-Bound $N = 23$ Cumulative Percentage	Place-Bound $N = 20$ Cumulative Percentage
1958	4	0
1959	22	0
1960	48	20
1961	70	55
1962	91	70
1963	91	85

ference in rate of adoption is evident year by year except for the first and last years on the table. The differences in the rate of adoption of modern math by the two types yielded a Mann-Whitney U score of 311 which has a p of .0228 on a one-tail test.

The superintendents also were asked about the adoption of five other educational innovations: language labs, team teaching, programmed instruction, foreign langauge instruction in the elementary grades, and accelerated programs in secondary education. Table 9–2 shows the

Table 9–2

NUMBER OF SELECTED INNOVATIONS ADOPTED BY 1963
BY TYPE OF SUPERINTENDENT

Number of Innovations Adopted	Career-Bound $N = 23$ Cumulative Percentage	Place-Bound $N = 20$ Cumulative Percentage
6	13	0
5 or more	30	10
4 or more	57	30
3 or more	78	45
2 or more	96	75
1 or more	100	100

relationship between type of superintendent and adoption of the six new practices.

Table 9–2 shows, as did Table 9–1, that place-bound superintendents lag behind career-bound superintendents in the adoption of new educational practices. The median number of innovations adopted was four for career-bound men and two for place-bound men. The difference in the number of adoptions of these six innovations by the two career types yielded a Mann-Whitney U score of 339 which has a p value of .004 on a one-tail test.

In both cases career-bound superintendents obviously have a faster rate of adoption of innovations than place-bound superintendents. The data show an evident difference in the rate of adoption of a single innovation, plus a significant difference in the number of innovations adopted over time. The cumulative effect of the unlike rates of acceptance of new practices can thus be seen.

Reynolds provides additional evidence of the difference. His sample consisted of 94 school systems in Illinois and Missouri. To measure rate of innovation he utilized a ratio of number of new practices adopted from a list of 31 new educational practices. The ratio was controlled to take into account the tenure of the school superintendent; he was credited only for what he adopted and the denominator of the ratio was reduced to correspond with the number of practices adopted by his predecessor. The mean innovativeness ratio for the 45 place-bound men was .0896 and was .1283 for the 49 career-bound men. The difference in the innovativeness scores produced an F-ratio of 18.15, significant at the .01 level on a one-tail test.[5]

Moreover, Reynolds provides striking data on the impact of length of time in office on the rate at which educational innovations are adopted. He collected data at the close of the 1964–65 school year on the number of innovations from a list of 31 adopted in that year as well as in the three preceding school years, 1963–64, 1962–63, and 1961–62.[6] Thus he obtained an adoption ratio performance record over four years for all men in his sample who had been in office at least five years. For the men who had been in office four years, he thus had a three-year adoption-ratio performance record. Likewise, he had a two-year adoption-ratio performance record for those in office for three years and a one-year record for those in office two years. Those in office for the first year at the time the data were gathered were dropped from the sample. By doing this Reynolds was able to answer the questions of the impact of tenure on the rate at which school superintendents adopt educational innovations. Figure 9–1 portrays the answer.

---

[5] Reynolds, "Innovation Related to Administrative Tenure, Succession, and Orientation," p. 66.

[6] Note again that the sample members were neither credited nor debited for the number of innovations on the list adopted by their predecessors.

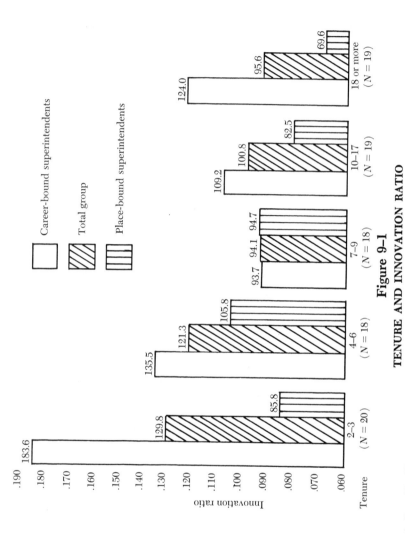

Figure 9–1

TENURE AND INNOVATION RATIO

Source: James A. Reynolds, "Innovation Related to Administrative Tenure, Succession, and Orientation" (Ph.D. diss., Washington University, 1965), Appendix E, Table 19, 135–37.

First, let's consider the innovation ratio over time of the total group. Note that it declines continually and that the drop is gradual. Thus the longer one has been in office, the lower his rate of adoption of educational innovations.

The differences between career- and place-bound superintendents is striking. While previously reported data have demonstrated a significant difference in rates of adoption between the two types of superintendents, the graph accents the differences. While the innovativeness ratio for career-bound superintendents declines over time and very sharply during the first few years in office, the ratio for place-bound superintendents begins at a relatively low level, rises somewhat and then, over time, gradually returns to its original low level. Note that the most marked differences in rate occur at the beginning of the term in office. Here we see that career-bound men have an adoption rate double that of place-bound men. This fact supports the notion that place-bound men take office devoid of a mandate for change. It underlines the notion that place-bound men are hired only when the school board is satisfied with the school system.

The works of Deprin and Knevlik confirm our findings. In his sample of ten superintendents new to their offices, Deprin found that in the first four years the five career-bound superintendents introduced 22 experimental educational projects while the five place-bound superintendents only introduced five.[7]

Knevlik's study concerned adoption rates in terms of origin of both the superintendent of the district and the origin of the high school principal. By way of conclusion, Knevlik stated:

> In this study, a strong relationship between administrative succession pattern and the frequency and extent of adoption of educational innovation [sic] was apparently due to the differences between outside and inside superintendents. While the investigation focused upon the principal and his orientation with the superintendent, there was no significant difference in the frequency and extent of adoption of new educational practices between outside and inside principals. In the test of the hypotheses, it was determined that only where there was a difference between outside and inside superintendents there occurred any significant difference in adoptions . . .
>
> School organizations appear to be more innovative, as measured by the adoption of new educational practices, in those instances

---

[7] Deprin, "Superintendent Succession and Administrative Patterns," p. 95.

where the administrative succession by superintendents has occurred from an origin outside the school system . . .[8]

The direct evidence that career-bound superintendents adopt more
educational innovations and at a faster pace than place-bound superintendents is fairly persuasive.[9] Indirect evidence is also supportive of
the finding. As shown in Chapter 4, career-bound men are more active
in communication about educational matters than are place-bound
men; and communication is necessary for adoption of innovations. In
his study of New York superintendents, Hickcox reports that 41 of the
303 career-bound men and 10 of the 170 place-bound men indicated
that they spent a great deal of time "keeping in touch with new trends,"
a difference statistically significant at the .10 level of confidence.[10]
Moreover, Hall has reported indirect evidence through the use of
adjectives which describe school systems. His research led him to
conclude:

> Superintendents who have been selected for their positions from
> outside the district administer programs and schools perceived by
> their staffs as more adaptable, dynamic, individualistic, and imagi-
> native than those administered by superintendents promoted from

---

[8] Stanley M. Knevlik, "The Effect of Administrative Succession Pattern Upon
Educational Innovation in Selected Secondary Schools" (Ph.D. diss., New York
University, 1967), pp. 92–93.

[9] Paul P. Preising, in "The Relationship of Staff Tenure and Administrative
Succession to Structural Innovation" (Ph.D. diss., Stanford University, 1968),
reports information about the origin of school superintendents and the adoption
of four educational innovations. In a sample of California schools he reports that
career-bound superintendents adopted significantly more of the innovations than
did place-bound superintendents. In a sample of Oregon schools his finding is in
the same direction but not statistically significant. It is surprising, however, that
Preising found statistically significant results. He apparently made a basic error
in the testing of his hypotheses. His sample consisted of 104 high schools in
Oregon and 308 in California. In the tests of the hypotheses relating to origin of
the superintendent and number of adoptions, he used 104 as the number of superintendents in Oregon and 308 as the number of superintendents in California. It
seems exceedingly unlikely that he drew only one high school from each school
district, though he is mum on the subject, and in fact never states how he arrived
at an adoption score for the superintendents. It appears then, for one thing, that
he seriously inflated the size of his sample of superintendents. Additionally, it
appears that he confounded the data, if indeed he did have more than one high
school per district, by permitting one superintendent, based on the adoption scores
of the various high schools in his district, to be placed in all three of his adoption
performance categories. Confounding the data in this manner renders the findings
virtually meaningless.

[10] Based on a secondary analysis of data in Hickcox, "Career and Place Bound
Orientations," p. 93.

within the system. Schools in districts administered by Inside Superintendents are perceived by their staffs as more stable, thorough, basic, reliable and disciplined than those administered by Outsiders. Teachers and principals serving under Insiders perceive their schools as more conservative and conventional while the staffs of Outsiders perceive their schools as more adaptable and forward-looking.[11]

---

[11] Hall, "Relations of Superintendents to Climate and Adaptability," 106–7.

10

Duration in Office

The preceding chapters have dealt with types of successors, their commitments, conditions of employment, and some of their early administrative activities. Emphasis has been placed on the beginning of the succession cycle, when the man is new to the particular position and is serving the first few years in office. This chapter focuses on the other end of the succession cycle—termination of stay in office and consequences for organizational development of the length of stay in office.

PERMANENCE AND EXPENDABILITY

The career of many superintendents is marked by movement from one community to another. Schools and superintendencies exist wherever people gather, and the potential places for employment are virtually unlimited. The basic problem which causes superintendents inevitably to move on has been but slightly overstated by Willard Waller.

We may say that the superintendent has a typical life history in the community. This typical life history repeats itself again and again in the life of one executive, and in the community with different executives. The life history seems to be about as follows: When the new executive takes charge of the school system, he has the support of nearly the entire community. . . . The board is usually with him to a man. This undivided support is his until some incident occurs which brings him into conflict with an individual or an organized group in the community. It is not long before such an incident occurs. . . . The essential weakness of his position is that it gives him an opportunity to make many more enemies than friends. Opportunities for becoming unpopular, to the point, almost, of infamy, are numerous, but opportunities for gaining friends are few.

. . . At the end of his first year, the superintendent has made some enemies, but the majority of the community, let us say, is still satisfied with the manner in which he is conducting the school. He has made some bitter enemies, as, apparently, he unavoidably must. . . . The superintendent has by now acquired certain enemies on the school board and they serve in the community as further radiant points of antagonism toward him. But the important fact, and the inexorable tragedy of the superintendent's life is that in the second year he usually makes a few more enemies, but he rarely has an opportunity to restore the balance by making friends of those who have previously been inimical to him. . . . Let us say that the superintendent has given the community a satisfactory school and that he is able at the end of the second year to win the fight. But if he does win at the end of the second year, he stands a greater chance of losing at the end of the third, for his position is continuously weakened. He makes more enemies than friends. And he makes decided enemies, if not bitter enemies, and only lukewarm friends.[1]

In their potential to move, some differences have been inferred about place-bound and career-bound superintendents and the subtypes. *Hoppers* move while there is still time, and before the completion of any major work started. They ride the tide and move when support wanes, and seem least able and interested in management of enemies. Only after he has completed his particular task does the *specialist* move. Once the task has been performed, his needs are no longer satisfied, and he seeks a new school system to start the whole performance over again. The *statesman* moves after he has exhausted his capabilities in a particular system.

---

[1] Willard Waller, *Sociology of Teaching* (New York: John Wiley & Sons, Inc., 1932), pp. 100–1.

All of these are subtypes within the category of career-bound. Moving is simply part of their career; they expect it. Thus career-bound superintendents look upon themselves as expendable. As one said: "I knew this was a tough job. It looked to me as if the school board and the system would have to go through one more superintendent before the several communities could learn to work together. I told the board this." When this superintendent resigned some time later, the local newspaper quoted him: "You hire a manager to do a job and if the team doesn't win, you don't look for excuses, you look for a new manager. There are 5,500 children involved here; the basic problems must be ironed out."

The place-bound superintendent seems best able to manage the enemies of which Waller spoke and is least mobile. Moving on does not fit into the place-bound superintendent's plans. As one remarked: "I've been in _____ a long time. I think I'm good 'till retirement. Besides, my wife wouldn't move." And in my presence, another place-bound man advised a subordinate as follows: "You're not too much younger than I am. I'm not going to leave here unless I have to, until I retire. You'll never be a superintendent here." The place-bound superintendent typically plans to retire from the position and defines his relationship to the position as permanent.

LENGTH OF INCUMBENCY AND ORIGIN OF SUPERINTENDENT

A place-bound superintendent's strong commitment to a community is made obvious by his remaining and waiting for the superintendency, thus implying he will stay in office longer than will a career-bound superintendent. Data gathered about differences in actual time spent in office prove this notion.

Data presented in Chapter 4 revealed that place-bound men look upon career movement with less favor than do career-bound superintendents; and that among men under 50, place-bound superintendents are significantly more inclined to express the desire to remain in their present superintendency until retirement. Moreover, a secondary analysis of raw data gathered by Seeman shows that attitudes toward mobility differ significantly between the two types. On a scale "whose purpose was to distinguish those for whom mobility interests take precedence over a wide range of more 'intrinsic' interests (for example, health, family, community)," [2] 11 place-bound superintendents scored

---

[2] Melvin Seeman, "Social Mobility and Administrative Behavior," p. 642.

a mean of 69.8 and 30 career-bound superintendents a mean of 78.5. The higher the score, the greater the interest in mobility.

Sample responses state: "I wouldn't let my friendship ties in a community stand in the way of moving on to a higher position." "The executive who has his eye on the jobs up the line, just can't go all out for the group he is serving at the moment." "My goal has always been to wind up as head of a small organization that I could guide over the long pull." "If you've got a worthwhile program developing in your present position, I don't think you ought to be really tempted if a bigger job comes your way." "If you stay quite a while in one executive position, you become too concerned with keeping things as they are." [3]

The differences in scores on the attitude toward mobility scale produced a z-score of 2.44 on the Mann-Whitney Test, significant beyond the .01 level on a one-tail test. These data, then, indicate that the place-bound superintendent is more inclined to hold onto the position; and they suggest that when he does terminate his stay in office, it is less in accord with his free will.

The secondary analysis of Seeman's data further shows that the mean time in office for place-bound superintendents was 8.3 years and 4.6 years for career-bound superintendents.

Table 10–1 shows the results of a secondary analysis of some ma-

Table 10–1

INCUMBENCY OF SUPERINTENDENTS

YEARS IN OFFICE	TYPE OF SUPERINTENDENT	
	Percentage of Place-Bound Superintendents ($N = 279$)	Percentage of Career-Bound Superintendents ($N = 513$)
1–2	14.3%	19.8%
3–4	16.5	17.7
5–9	23.0	28.2
10–14	23.6	21.4
15–19	6.8	6.8
20–24	7.2	1.8
25 and over	6.5	4.0

Source: Secondary analysis of raw data gathered for AASA, *Profile of the School Superintendent*.

---

[3] *Ibid.*, pp. 635, 641.

terial from the American Association of School Administrators' survey of characteristics of superintendents. It indicates the length of incumbency and origin of 792 superintendents. About 44 per cent of the place-bound superintendents have held the job ten or more years and about 34 per cent of the career-bound superintendents have been in one superintendency that long. The mean time in office in this sample for place-bound men was ten years and eight years for career-bound men. The difference in terms in office of the two types yields a chi-square value of 20.9 with 6 *df.*, significant at the .005 level on a one-tail test.

The distribution of types of superintendents by time in office in a sample of 798 superintendents from Oregon, Allegheny County, Pennsylvania, West Virginia, Massachusetts, and New York is shown in Table 10–2. In this sample the mean number of years in office is 7.9

Table 10–2

INCUMBENCY OF SUPERINTENDENTS

TYPE OF SUPERINTENDENT	NUMBER OF YEARS IN OFFICE					
	1	2–5	6–10	11–15	16–20	21 or more
Career-Bound ($N = 473$)	61	181	101	54	39	37
Place-Bound ($N = 325$)	31	88	63	61	42	40

for career-bound superintendents and 10.2 for place-bound superintendents. Again the difference is statistically significant: the distribution yields a chi-square value of 25.8 with 5 degrees of freedom, significant at the .0005 level of confidence on a one-tail test.[4]

LENGTH OF INCUMBENCY AND ORGANIZATIONAL DEVELOPMENT

What consequences, then, does the length of time a man stays in one superintendency have for the development of that school system? Can

---

[4] Similarly, Gordon Samson reports as a result of a study of administrative tenure in 737 school systems in the Midwest, "Boards in low-turnover districts tend to promote a person from within the system to the position of superintendent." See M. E. Stapley, *School Board Studies* (Chicago: Midwest Administration Center, University of Chicago, 1957), p. 39.

school superintendents stay too long or move too soon? School superintendents have definite ideas about these questions. Like city managers,[5] school superintendents assert that they can hurt the profession and fail to render proper service by moving too soon or by staying too long. The *hopper,* for example, is thought by superintendents to move too soon.

On the other end of the scale, one superintendent has written: "If a man stayed in one administrative post for very many years, he must be tremendously efficient and capable, or else resort to the practice of job self-perpetuation at the expense of any creditable educational performance in his district." [6] Expanding on the same theme while making a plea for longer contracts another superintendent has written:

> To be all things he should be as a professional, and to be the politician he must be to win the votes [of the school board] necessary for re-election, is asking a great deal of a man. Perhaps too much. Sooner or later, to secure another contract, he becomes more political than professional. . . . Who then, can blame a superintendent if he becomes a politician, a fence-straddler, a man who puts his own welfare and that of his own children ahead of his educational principles . . . a temporizer, a person slow to take a definite stand for what he knows is right, lest he makes some powerful enemies.[7]

The actions of one California superintendent who did not make too many enemies, won many re-elections, and stayed too long, have been reported in a case study by James Stewart. The man who Stewart calls "Setwell" was a place-bound superintendent who had served about 27 years in a system with over 7,000 pupils. The "ingredients of administrative longevity" cited in the case were:

> (1) Setwell never permitted himself to take a position in conflict with his Board of Education. (2) He made the selection of new members of the Board of Education [who were appointed by the mayor] a matter of vital concern to himself and normally succeeded in exerting significant influence in the naming of the new members. (3) Setwell's relationship with many members of the Board transcended the official relationship. (4) [He] was normally

---

[5] See G. K. Floro, "Continuity in City Manager Careers," *American Journal of Sociology,* Vol. 61 (November, 1955), 240–46.

[6] T. H. Bell, *The Prodigal Pedagogue* (New York: Exposition Press, 1955), p. 149.

[7] H. M. Barr, "Should Superintendents Be Gypsies?" *American School Board Journal,* Vol. 122 (February, 1951), 36–37.

adroit in his ability to avoid conflict-producing situations. (5) Setwell was an active member of essentially every community organization for which he was eligible. (6) He befriended hundreds of individuals in ways which created in them a feeling of personal indebtedness to him. (7) He made himself readily available for service in the multitude of community projects. (8) He carefully maintained personal contact with students in the schools, creating among them in each generation an affection for him. (9) Setwell had a reputation among colleagues and laymen of being a person . . . who did not 'fall for every fad that came along' and who felt that the 'three R's' were of basic significance. (10) He seldom attempted to influence teaching methods or to organize in-service education . . . (11) He was known to the teachers as a person who would not 'press for better salaries' for teachers and to the business community as a person 'who did not insist that all money go for teachers' salaries.' (12) Throughout his career he enjoyed the confidence of the more prominent and influential elements of the community. (13) He survived a politically motivated attempt to remove him from office and emerged from the conflict a popular hero. (14) In his younger days Setwell was an athlete and a successful coach, a fact which was remembered affectionately by many and which gave him a contact with still another facet of the community. (15) He was a 'politician,' both in the sense that he could distinguish the possible from the impossible and in the sense that he was willing to sacrifice principle for expediency when he thought the larger good would thus be served. (16) Although his relationships with his subordinate administrators were notable for their excellence, the relationships were that of father and son. Decisions of importance were made by Setwell, not by conference. (17) Setwell was sensitive to the 'picture' of him carried in the mind of persons in the community. He, therefore, carefully constructed this picture, producing what can only be described as a legend, which depicted his activities in a highly entertaining and complimentary way. (18) He was a person of rare personal magnitude, a speaker of outstanding ability, and a raconteur of exceptional skill.[8]

What is included in this list of factors is no more significant than what is *not* included. The list is completely void of laudatory, positive statements about Setwell's contributions to the development of the school system during his 27-year reign.

A similar relation between performance and tenure in office has been observed about mental hospital superintendents. Belknap wrote:

---

[8] James I. Stewart, "The Career of a School Superintendent: A Case Study of Administrative Longevity" (Ph.D. diss., Stanford University, 1954), pp. 158ff.

... The superintendents have been confronted, as medical men, with a dilemma. If they conformed to the structure of the hospital as they found it, they could carry out a reasonably good, routine custodial administration. If, however, they attempted to establish modern psychiatric treatment of patients, the procedures necessary called for changes in the traditional routines ... But the professional training of any physician has been for at least the past hundred years in the direction of seeking and finding improvement in the condition of his patients. ... The superintendents ... found themselves confronted with a choice between being good doctors and poor administrators, or good administrators and poor doctors. ... The superintendents with the longest tenure were those who apparently accepted the second horn of the dilemma and became efficient administrators.[9]

Aside from these expressions of the feeling that a long stay in office by the superintendent is detrimental to the development of the school system, there exists striking evidence. As shown in the preceding chapter, the evidence indicates that the innovativeness of the school systems decline progressively the longer the superintendent stays in office.

All offices must eventually change hands, and with school superintendencies, the switch is frequent. Superintendents have infinitely more chances to make enemies than friends, and they must be re-elected by an ever-changing school board; thus they do not ordinarily last long even if they want to. And according to superintendents, a man can insure lengthy tenure only if he is more "political" than "professional."

Superintendents consider a long tenure detrimental to the development of the school system. They see a dilemma; they realize that a school superintendent cannot act in a manner that assures re-election over and over while systematically developing the quality of the educational service rendered by the school district. The sharper the focus on the one alternative, the less attention given to the other.

The fact that place-bound men stay in office longer than career-bound men infers that those promoted from within give more attention to being re-elected and less to developing the school system than do those promoted to the superintendency from outside.

---

[9] From pp. 79–80, *Human Problems in a State Mental Hospital* by Ivan Belknap. Copyright 1956, McGraw-Hill Book Company. Used with permission of McGraw-Hill Book Company.

11

The Successor's Successor

In a sense, this analysis has partially followed two hypothetical school systems through the succession cycle of the chief executive. It has followed some of the events from the time the new superintendent is elected until his term in office ends. It has been demonstrated that when a school board, in hiring a new superintendent, judges that the schools have been functioning at a level below that expected or desired, it reaches outside the containing organization for the new executive; only when the school board is satisfied with the way the schools are functioning will it take on a new chief executive from within the containing organization.

Men who wait within the containing organization to be appointed its chief executive—men promoted from within— have been labeled place-bound. They attach more value to the place of employment than they do to their career, thus they wait for the superintendency to come to them. Men who do not wait—those who seek the superintendency outside their containing organization—have been labeled career-bound. By seeking a superintendency away from the home system, they indicate that a higher value is attached to the career than to the place of employment.

Career- and place-bound superintendents not only differ

in the value they attach to the career of a superintendent, they also exhibit different career styles. Though the picture is slightly over-drawn, it is apparent that once in the occupational field of education the career-bound superintendent sets his sights early and high, and considers positions below the superintendent as rungs up to the su-perintendency. In preparing for his career he is active; he receives his graduate training early, to the fullest extent, and from the "better" universities.

The place-bound superintendent, on the other hand, traces a career which seems to be typified by gradually escalating occupational as-pirations. He raises his aspirations as he successfully fills positions of increasing responsibility until one day he finds himself in the superin-tendency. He is less active than his counterpart in preparing for the career; he tends to drag out the period of formal education and to ac-quire less than the maximum possible formal education, and to secure it from universities of modest quality. Moreover, the place-bound su-perintendent is less progressive in his views about schooling than is his counterpart and he does not aspire to prominence in this chosen field like the career-bound man.

Career- and place-bound superintendents also occupy different posi-tions in the social structure of school superintendents. Place-bound men hold lower status in the social order and are less involved in the social network of interaction than are career-bound superintendents. In addi-tion, the vital flow of information about educational practices is largely managed by career-bound superintendents. Furthermore, elected of-fices in the American Association of School Administrators are held more often, in proportion to the numbers, by career-bound men.

A school board, dissatisfied with the performance of the schools, hires a career-bound superintendent and gives him a mandate for change. Only when the school board is satisfied does it hire a place-bound man. And under this condition, no mandate for change is given.

Taken together, the differing conditions of employment of the two types of superintendents, their differing career styles, and the different positions they hold in the social structure of superintendents produce different performances by career- and place-bound superintendents. Over-all, their performance fulfills the conditions of employment; the career-bound superintendent is far more active than the place-bound superintendent in making alterations in staff, policies, and educational programs.

The performances of the two types of school superintendents are so different it is bound to have a bearing on the kind of men selected to follow them in office. To bring the analysis full circle, it is necessary to show that the performances of career- and place-bound superintendents are related to the type of their successors. This will be done through an examination of succession patterns.

TWO PLACE-BOUND SUPERINTENDENTS IN A ROW MIGHT BE ONE TOO MANY

The differences between the ways the two types of superintendents relate to their containing organizations are sufficiently marked to suggest the proposition that a school system cannot afford two place-bound men in a row. With two in a row, a school system would average about 20 years of maintenance of the status quo. This is a longer period of this type of leadership than most school districts can afford. During such a period, adaptation and development would lag; a reputation would circulate that little of interest occurs in the district and thus able people would not be attracted; the public would complain about outmoded procedures and practices; and institutional integrity would suffer because the place-bound superintendent is seemingly more willing to make compromises.

Four possible succession patterns exist for the two types: place-bound to place-bound, place-bound to career-bound, career-bound to career-bound, and career-bound to place-bound. On the basis of what has been indicated above, it would be expected that the pattern of place-bound to place-bound would rarely occur. Study of 103 successions taking place over about 32 years in 48 city school systems in California revealed that the least frequent pattern of succession was from place-bound to place-bound. This pattern occurred only 7 times among the 103 instances of succession. A study of succession patterns in school districts of Pennsylvania replicated the finding. Table 11–1 gives the findings of both samples.

In the combined samples of 209 instances of succession, there were 16 cases of place-bound to place-bound succession. Six of these took place in three of the 89 districts.

The fact that the pattern of place-bound to place-bound succession occurs only infrequently supports the proposition that normally a school system cannot afford two place-bound superintendents in a row. In addition, it further validates the finding that place-bound superintendents tend to be appointed only when the school board is satisfied with the way the schools are being administered.

Additional support for this proposition comes from an examination of what happens to an organization that has had two place-bound chief

Table 11–1

SUCCESSION PATTERNS

SUCCESSION PATTERN	CALIFORNIA [*]	PENNSYLVANIA [**]
Career-Bound to Career-Bound	58	43
Place-Bound to Place-Bound	7	9
Career-Bound to Place-Bound	22	31
Place-Bound to Career-Bound	16	23
Total	103	106

[*] Data gathered for all (48) city school districts in California from the annual directory of California Association of Secondary Administrators, California Schools, for the period 1926 to 1958.

[**] Data gathered for all (24) first- and second-class school districts and 17 third-class districts in Pennsylvania drawn at random from personnel files in the State Department of Public Instruction for the period 1922 to 1959.

executives in a row. An example is available that deals with a business firm. Placing the problem not on the origin of the successor, but on the practice of replacing the chief executive at the last moment and in a haphazard fashion, Christiansen reports:

> The selection of the new general manager at the last moment and without preparation has, in extreme cases, produced some very capable leaders; it has also produced some very poor executives who have run their firms into serious trouble. More frequently the result has been the selection of a man who manages the company by letting it continue pretty much 'as is,' with little change in policies or procedures, little questioning or review of established objectives and competitive niche. The change in top management has not been used as an opportunity to reappraise but rather to continue past tradition. The cases of the Burgess Boiler Works, the Diamond Mine Light Company, and the Food Processing Corporation point up the results of such a situation.
>
> The Burgess Boiler Works had grown steadily after its founding in 1902. Originally a boiler repair shop, the company had expanded into the fabrication, erection, and repair of boilers throughout the central Ohio region. In 1914 the Burgess family sold its stock to a group of investors, and Mr. Taylor, the company's sales manager, was made president and general manager. Mr. Taylor's vigorous direction resulted in expansion in terms of sizes, types, and numbers of boilers produced, and also in new lines involving metal shaping and forming. Annual sales reached a peak of $2 million in 1924. In the next year Mr. Stubbs replaced Mr. Taylor after

the latter retired. Mr. Stubbs had been the company's chief engineering estimator for many years and had a very thorough knowledge of boiler construction and engineering.

Under Mr. Stubbs' administration, as well as that of his successor, Mr. Alger, the company stood still. In 1952 dollar sales had risen somewhat over 1924, but unit sales had declined. Profits had been adequate but not strong. Company equipment, buildings, and management were old but all in good running order. Ignoring advances in boiler design and the development of new metals that could be used successfully in both boiler and tank construction, the Burgess Company continued to concentrate on its standard line of small boilers and tanks for institutional and commercial use. This field continued to offer Burgess a steady source of profitable business. Management's policy of just holding the line was illustrated during World War II when Mr. Alger turned down an Armed Forces offer of technical and financial help to expand in tank and vessel work because he was not sure just what problems such a move would create.

Burgess, under Mr. Stubbs and Mr. Alger, let slip its opportunities both to expand old lines and to invade new fields. As general managers, Mr. Stubbs and Mr. Alger lacked the ability to do more than just keep the company going. Both men had been effective in their former positions as heads of the Burgess engineering division, but neither had received any special coaching or training to prepare him for more complicated duties. Management succession for Burgess had been handled by waiting until a replacement was needed, then by promoting some member of the current executive group to the vacant top position. The method of selecting a leader was adequate to keep the company in business but did not permit it to forge ahead in the vanguard of competition.[1]

Similar evidence about public schools supports the proposition.[2] An exploratory study in a large school system which, in its rather recent

---

[1] C. Roland Christansen, *Management Succession in Small and Growing Enterprises* (Boston: Graduate School of Business Administration, Harvard University, 1953), pp. 24–25.

[2] In a study of the development of a newly created junior college, Burton Clark made note of the fact that all administrators of the college came from positions within the public school system. (In California, a junior college such as the one involved in the study, is frequently operated and maintained by what is the usual school system and thus is an extension of the public school system to include the first two years of a college program.) Concluding his comments about the practice of promotion from within Clark said: "... The district selection of 'district men' to administer the college is a clear example of what might generally be known as *restraint by recruitment*. The district attempted to secure conformity to district and

past, had three place-bound superintendents in a row was made. The informants universally reported that the three men "just kept the schools going." No informant could recall a single noticeable change made by the three. The emphasis of the schools, its curriculum, way of organizing grades, and methods of internal administration were unaltered. A pattern was set by the superintendent who preceded these three place-bound men and that pattern was never seriously questioned, but simply followed.

In addition to supporting the proposition, this exploration indicated the conditions under which such a succession pattern occurs. The pattern centers around a man who will be called Adam. Adam had served four years as superintendent of schools before resigning to enter the real estate business in the community. Adam and his successor, Baker, were career-bound men. Baker served seven years and died in office. Baker was considered an outstanding superintendent and his pattern for the school system was followed by the three place-bound men, Carlisle, Douglas, and Ford. Each stayed from six to eight years, and two terminated their stay in office prematurely because of illness or death. The third took a job with a book company. Adam and Baker shared a concern for business education and the school program reflected their interest: both Carlisle and Ford came to the superintendency from the business department of the school system.

These factors seem to account for the pattern of three place-bound men in a row:

(1) *Stable and Dominated School Board* Three years after Adam resigned from the superintendency he was elected to the school board and held office until defeated in the primaries some 24 years later. Because he had been superintendent, many board members looked to him for guidance. From the beginning he was a dominant force on the board; in fact, many said he *was* the board.

During Adam's tenure on the board, its membership was very stable. Three of the nine members who served while Adam was superintendent were still on the school board twenty years later when Ford was ap-

---

public school norms through selection of men with appropriate backgrounds. The uniformity of the backgrounds would also help to produce homogeneity of outlook. These restraints were not fully controlling and deviation from the desired norms did occur. But the general effect of the district's form of recruitment was to give the administration of the college a public school cast and to restrain somewhat the tendency for the college to go its own way." From p. 112, *The Open Door College: A Case Study* by Burton R. Clark. Copyright 1960, McGraw-Hill Book Company. Used with permission of McGraw-Hill Book Company.

pointed superintendent. Counting Adam himself, this made four with a long history of service.

(2) *Conservatism*   Adam, who reportedly dominated the board, was conservative, as can be seen from the following statement he had printed in a local paper regarding school finances.

> The school system also must be given time to catch its breath before extending its services into new fields. There are times when it takes the stoutest hearts to hold the line. I want to see that line held. To venture on forward movements at this time would be an act of warped delusive judgment. On the other hand, retreats are marked by the confusion and the disorder that prevails when fear reigns. The safe course is the middle course—holding the line . . .

(3) *Party Politics*   Evidence suggested that city politics were inseparable from school-board operations. The board was Republican during Adam's time. The fact that he was defeated in the primaries marks it as a political rather than a popular defeat. Most informants reported that to get a job, noncertified personnel needed to belong to the "right" party. And the school system developed a reputation of having more custodians and other service personnel per pupil than any system in the state.

It was suggested by several people that the place-bound men were appointed to the superintendency because of their business education interest and as a reward for political loyalty. During Ford's term in office the political makeup of the board changed. Adam was one of the last remaining Republicans. The changed school board called on a career-bound superintendent when Ford could no longer hold office.

The factors that account for the succession pattern of place-bound to place-bound in this one school system do not exhaust all explanations. It is always possible that one man is a deviant member of his type. It may also be that a school district takes on another place-bound man because it did not receive the full impact of the first's potential because his term in office was cut short by death or a similar incapacitating event. Anyway, the exploration in the one school district exhibiting the pattern, the noted differences in the performances of the two types, and the fact that such succession occurs infrequently, indicates that this kind of succession pattern can be "explained." In addition, evidence can be found to show that the conditions of the school district at the given period were unique.

The 16 instances of place-bound to place-bound succession in the school superintendency in 209 cases raises the question of what might be found in other kinds of organizations. Comparative data are lacking, but the differences in the relationships of various kinds of organizations to their environments seem to suggest what the data might reveal.

Darwin and Wallace pointed out long ago that under changing conditions, the importance of adaptation on the part of an organism cannot be overstated. In their account the organism is in a stern battle for survival; those that do not adapt do not survive. Darwin and Wallace had reference to animals in their natural state; however, they did point out that varieties tended to return to the original form in a domesticated setting where the environment is stable. Survival, in this setting, is not a challenge, and adaptation is thus not crucial. The point is not that organizations and organisms are alike in all respects, but that public schools in comparison to other organizations can be said to be domesticated and thus have less need to adapt to the environment.

They are domesticated in the sense they are not compelled to attend to all of their needs. For example, a steady flow of clients is assured. There is no fight for survival in this class of organizations. Though public schools do compete for resources, support is not dependent on or closely tied to quality of performance. The business firm in a competitive industry, on the other hand, can be said to exist in a wild setting. They do struggle for survival. Such a business firm is not protected at vulnerable points as is the public school system.

It is reasonable, then, to argue that the closer an organization is toward the domesticated end of the continuum, the better it can survive the impact of two place-bound men in a row; and the closer an organization is to the wild end of the continuum, the less able it will be to survive beyond two place-bound men in a row.

The Longer the Term in Office the Greater the Probability of a Career-Bound Successor

The data suggest another proposition about performance in office and its relationship to the type of successor. School superintendents, as indicated before, see a long tenure in office as detrimental to the development of a school system. They say that if a man stays in office a long time the schools will deteriorate because the long term means the superintendent has been devoting more effort to being re-elected than to the development of the school system. And when the administration of the schools is deemed to be unsatisfactory at a time for replacement, school boards seek a new superintendent from outside the containing organization. Thus it is to be expected that, when a man stays a long time in office, the board will call on a career-bound superintendent to be his replacement. This suggests the proposition that if a man's stay in office is long, the chances are greater that his replacement will be a career-bound man than if his stay in office is short.

What constitutes a long term in office? The AASA survey found the mean time in office of 859 superintendents to be 9.1 years. Thus a *long term* in office can be defined as one lasting 10 or more years. On this basis, then, the data revealed that when superintendents' terms in office were short, 62 per cent of the successors were career-bound. And when superintendents' terms in office were long (10 or more years) 73 per cent of the successors were career-bound. Therefore, chances are 62 out of 100 that the successor of a short-term superintendent will be career-bound and 73 out of 100 that the successor of a man who had a long term in office will be career-bound.

Table 11–2 shows the percentage of career-bound successors with predecessors' terms in office divided into five-year spans. With the exception of the span from 16 to 20 years (which remains a great curiosity) the table shows the continual increase in the percentage of career-bound successors with the increase of time spent in office by the predecessors.

Table 11–2

LENGTH OF TERM IN OFFICE AND TYPE OF SUCCESSOR

YEARS IN OFFICE OF PREDECESSORS	NUMBER OF PLACE-BOUND SUCCESSORS	NUMBER OF CAREER-BOUND SUCCESSORS	PER CENT OF CAREER-BOUND SUCCESSORS
1–5	25	38	60
6–10	18	37	67
11–15	7	26	79
16–20	12	8	40
21 and over	1	14	93

STATESMEN ARE FOLLOWED BY PLACE-BOUND SUPERINTENDENTS

A third proposition about the successor's successor dealing with a subtype of career-bound superintendent can be derived from the data. Interviews with school superintendents revealed that there was a type recognized for superior performance. In part, his performance was distinguishable because he demonstrated concern for all phases of the educational program and for the long-run consequences of administrative acts. This kind of superintendent terminated his stay in office not because he succumbed to the lure of a fresh start in a new place or because he had completed a specialized task, but because he felt he had exhausted his capabilities in improving the school system. This type of superintendent was called a *statesman*.

Because superintendents consider his performance highly admirable, and because he leaves only when he feels that he has reached the limit of his capabilities, the inference that the statesman will leave the schools in such a condition that the school board will deem that they are being satisfactorily administered seems logical. If this is the case, then it is to be expected that statesmen will be followed in the superintendency by place-bound men to a greater extent than would be expected on the basis of chance. This is true. It can be demonstrated from the succession pattern data and succession histories surrounding some statesmen.[3]

To determine if place-bound men succeeded statesmen to a greater extent than chance would indicate, three knowledgeable judges submitted names of people who exhibited the characteristics of statesmen and who were serving or had served in their state during the last 40 years. At least two of the three judges agreed on 24 individuals.

These 24 statesmen had terminated their services in 36 superintendencies in small, medium, and large school systems; therefore, as a group, they had been followed into office by 36 successors. The successors of these statesmen consisted of 21 place-bound and 15 career-bound men. Chance expectations indicate that about 12 of the 36 successors should be place-bound and about 24 should be career-bound—for about one-third of the school superintendents are promoted from within. The difference between the extent to which statesmen are followed by place-bound men and chance expectations is in the direction predicted and beyond the .01 level of confidence. Thus it is clear that statesmen tend to be followed in the superintendency by individuals promoted from within.[4]

---

[3] In a similar vein Dale has noted that leadership shifts from entrepreneurial types to managerial types. See Ernest Dale, "Contributions to Administration by Alfred P. Sloan, Jr., and G. M.," *Administrative Science Quarterly*, Vol. 1 (June, 1956), 30–62.

[4] The marked tendency for the statesman type of superintendent to be replaced by someone from within the school system recalls the theory of the "circulation of elites" to which it seemingly has some relationship. From Pareto's discussion of the circulation of elites, "we are offered the hypothesis that innovator types (the 'Foxes') are needed to devise new programs and techniques. To be effective, these

The Successor's Successor

The concepts of place-bound and career-bound superintendents have proved useful in predicting the central pattern of action in the way the two types of successors relate to their containing school system. The differences in patterns of actions and relationships to the organization permit a tentative characterization of the two types. The unlike performances label the place-bound superintendent as an adaptive man and the career-bound superintendent as an innovator. Both are conformists in the sense that they turn in a performance in keeping with the essential conditions of employment. But there is a marked difference. The place-bound man adapts or modifies himself to fit the office; his performance adds nothing new to the role. It is not creative. It is a stabilizing performance aimed at preserving the status quo. The place-bound superintendent seems to derive status from the office; he does not bring status to it. He is like an understudy, a stand-in or stand-by. When called on, he takes the place of the predecessor as opposed to replacing him. In a sense he inherits the office and performs within a framework already established.

The performance of the career-bound superintendent, on the other hand, does add something to the role. He is neither an understudy nor an inheritor. With succession from outside, the office rather than the person is modified. His performance changes the office and the relations of others to the office; therefore, it has been called creative.

The latent roles of the two types equip them for their unlike performances. The place-bound superintendent, wanting to stay in the community, adapts himself to survive. The career-bound superintendent does not necessarily want to stay; he is more committed to the occupation than to the place in which it is performed.

It is important to stress that the concepts and predictions were not based, or directly dependent on, individual personality traits of successors. In other words, it is possible to predict the central pattern of action

---

'Foxes' must be associated with more conservative, forceful elements having strong institutional loyalties and perseverance. As the new system or institution gains strength and has something to defend, the 'Foxes' become more expendable; and the 'Lions' take over complete control, trimming innovations to meet the needs of survival. But this in turn may limit adaptation to new conditions. The institutional problem is to keep a proper balance of the social types needed at each stage. This theory might well be salvaged and reformulated in more workaday terms for use in the study of specific institutions, including administrative structures, rather than of whole societies and historical epochs." Philip Selznick, *Leadership in Administration* (Evanston, Ill.: Row Peterson and Company, 1957), p. 112. Used by permission.

of a successor in the office of the superintendent simply on the basis of his origin in reference to the containing organization. Moreover, place- and career-bound superintendents differ in no significant way on personality measures such as Gough's California Psychological Inventory, the California F Scale, Rokeach's Dogmatism Scale, the Pensacola Z Scale, and the Allport-Vernon-Lindzey Study of Values. The lack of personality differences seems understandable in light of the homogeneity of superintendents; they represent a compressed age range, they are all males, they are all married, they have obtained similar amounts of formal education, and they are all in the same occupation. This is not to say that the individual personality characteristics of the successor are unimportant regarding his performance and its consequences. It is hardly to be questioned that personality factors are important in executive's roles. But the over-all pattern of action of the successor is predictable simply from his origin.

What the concepts suggest is that the central pattern in the performance in office of place- and career-bound superintendents is governed by a configuration of mutual expectations about the role to be played and by forces external to the individual. To borrow some phrases which are current and cover the essential meaning, the performances of the two types are simply matters of taking one's proper station [5] or the definition of the situation.[6]

The individual, therefore, is not totally free to define for himself the way he will perform in the position of superintendent of schools. Certainly, many aspects of the performance are under his control. But the central pattern of his performance tends to be beyond his reach and is set by his origin in respect to the containing organization.

In a similar vein, McGee's study of differential treatment of faculty members at the University of Texas shows that even though those who hold Texas Ph.D.'s spend a longer period of time in the lower academic ranks and have heavier teaching loads than those with Ph.D.'s from other institutions, "there is no reason to believe that the differential treatment of the inbred product is the result of inferior quality on his part." [7]

It has often been said that the school board's most important function is to select a school superintendent. And the data presented here sug-

---

[5] See Ruth Benedict, *The Chrysanthemum and the Sword* (Boston: Houghton Mifflin Company, 1946), pp. 43–75.

[6] See W. I. Thomas, in *Social Behavior and Personality*, E. H. Volkart (ed.), (New York: Social Science Research Council, 1951), pp. 226–31.

[7] See Reece McGee, "The Function of Institutional Inbreeding," *American Journal of Sociology*, Vol. 65 (March, 1960), 483–88.

gest that the central pattern of action of the successor can be predicted in advance based on the origin of the successor. If the school board chooses a successor from within the containing organization, the central tendency of his performance will be to stabilize what exists; if the school board reaches outside the containing school system for a successor, the central tendency of his performance will be to alter what exists.

To make an over-all case for or against the employment of a career- or place-bound successor on the basis of these data would be presumptuous. Their patterns of action are different. They do turn in unlike performances in the office; this is clear. However, there are periods in the life cycle of an organization when change is needed as well as periods when change is undesirable. Thus, no easy answer about the successor's successor in the superintendency is available. The data, nevertheless, further highlight the important function of the school board—the selection of a school superintendent. In that the origin of the new chief executive serves as a clear indicator of the central tendency of his performance in office, the school board, by hiring one of the two types, is at least in the position to determine whether the school system is to change in some way or is to maintain itself and firm up what exists.